Michael Collins

From a
Fibreglass Hull

with illustrations by the author

ADLARD COLES LIMITED
GRANADA PUBLISHING
London Toronto Sydney New York

Charles Scribner's Sons New York

Published by Granada Publishing in
Adlard Coles Limited, 1979

Granada Publishing Limited
Frogmore, St Albans, Herts AL2 2NF
and
3 Upper James Street, London W1R 4BP
Suite 405, 4th Floor, United Nations Plaza, New York, NY 10017, USA
Q164 Queen Victoria Buildings, Sydney, NSW 2000, Australia
100 Skyway Avenue, Toronto, Ontario, Canada M9W 3A6
PO Box 84165, Greenside, 2034, Johannesburg, South Africa
CML Centre, Queen and Wyndham, Auckland 1, New Zealand

Copyright © 1979 by Michael Collins

ISBN 0 229 11616 7

Printed in Great Britain by
Fletcher and Son Ltd, Norwich

Published in the United States by
Charles Scribner's Sons, 1979
ISBN 0 229 11616 7

Contents

Introduction

As the cost of purchasing complete new craft soars ever higher, the idea of completing one's own boat based on a standard fibreglass hull becomes more attractive to many practically minded yachtsmen.

However, it should be borne in mind that successful completion of such a project depends on a high level of practical ability and application. The work involved, for both power and sailing boats, ranges through joinery, plumbing, engineering, electrical work, painting and a few combinations of these. In this respect some amateur builders are able to 'sub-contract' those parts of the work with which they are least familiar to suitably accomplished friends or professionals.

It is not the aim of this book to be a technical reference on the finer arts of the above trades, but merely a guide to the key points for setting the project off and running the work through in logical sequence. We will assume that the builder is reasonably competent and that the hull to be fitted out is between twenty and thirty feet in length.

I

Choosing your Boat

Before considering building, any prospective owner will have fairly clear ideas on which type of boat he wants. This desire must of course, be tempered by other factors, principally the depth of his pocket and the availability of a suitable building site.

Some suppliers of fibreglass mouldings are able to offer a comprehensive list of kit parts including all joinery, fastenings, materials, engines, spars, sails etc. to complete the vessel. From this information it is easy to assess a budget to cover the whole job, and this could possibly be spread over the period of the building. If this period is extended, you will have to take inflation into account also.

Do not be misled when looking at advertisements for hulls in the magazines which say 'hulls from a certain price'. This often means just what is says: the bare hull. You must check what 'extras' are actually essentials such as keel, deck and superstructure, hatches, internal mouldings, rudder, engine beds and so on. These are often not included in the basic price. Generally, if you buy the hull with deck, superstructure, rudder and ballast keel fitted, the cost of completing the vessel will be between two and three times that initial outlay, depending on the extent of the equipment you choose to fit. This rough estimate applies to both power and sailing craft.

Before any hard and fast decisions are made, visit a few moulders to see some hulls, so that you can compare value for money and the quality of their workmanship. There are usually a few hulls in their yards that you can inspect.

Firstly, walk around the hull, looking along the sides from various angles to observe the fairness of its shape. Any imperfections show themselves up by apparent wobbles in the reflections of light on its surface.

Try to discover how thick the hulls are; you may not be able to see much to indicate this, so press against the sides to observe any undue amount of flexing, and enquire about the thickness. As a guide, the hull of a 30ft sailing boat should be a minimum of $\frac{1}{2}$in thick near the keel, thinning to about $\frac{3}{8}$in on the topsides, possibly with some reinforcement in stressed areas such as engine beds, rigging etc. Make sure there are no blow holes in the gel coat surface, particularly near corners. This is caused by poor mixing or poor application technique.

The hull is often made in two halves which are trimmed along their joining faces before being brought together and bonded over on the inside. Have a look for the join both inside and out. You should not be able to see it either side, but check that the laminates everywhere are neat and thoroughly bonded to the two halves.

Look at the stringers inside the hull. These are strips of plastic foam placed around the hull and bonded over to form longitudinal box stiffening. Look for reinforced areas at highly stressed points such as where the chainplates are to be fitted. The inside surface of the hull should be well covered with resin with no fibres exposed. It should be an even grey colour with no silvery looking areas, which would indicate that insufficient resin has been used in the laminating process; this is known as being 'resin shy'. A well finished hull with adequate stringers and reinforcement will be integrally strong.

Some designers, particularly of racing craft, omit some or all of these reinforcements. They specify instead that the joinery, when bonded-in, is to form the integral stiffness required. Whilst this method is acceptable, it puts the responsibility on the finisher to achieve the required strength.

You will need to decide at this stage whether you want any of the work to be done in advance by the supplier. Do any bulkheads, internal mouldings or head linings have to go in before the deck is fitted? Getting this preliminary work done by the moulder is often a big advantage for the amateur builder. Consider at this point how you will lift the engine into the hull safely, and how you will fit a ballast keel at home. The problems can be overcome simply and economically by forward planning, so that the time and money they involve does not come as a nasty surprise later on.

It is usual to buy a hull with the deck and superstructure fitted, because lifting the superstructure into place at home is difficult. The superstructure stiffens the top of the hull and ensures that it is the correct shape; this is an advantage in transporting and unloading. The more expensive hulls are sometimes offered with fibreglass headlinings fitted to the inside of the superstructure before it is attached to the topsides. If you can afford them, they are well worthwhile, saving a lot of work later.

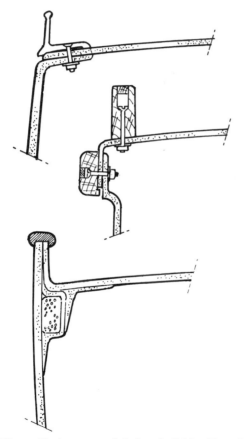

Fig 1   *Various types of deck to hull join. Top: deck bedded, bolted and bonded to hull flange and fitted with an alloy toe rail. Middle: deck which caps over the hull and is then fitted with a wood toe rail. Bottom: well deck moulding, bedded on a shelf and bonded over inside. This forms the toe rail which is then fitted with a capping.*

The deck to hull joint is bedded in either mastic or resin putty, bolted through at intervals and bonded over thoroughly on the inside (see fig 1). Whoever is to tackle this job must do it well, because a weak or leaky join will be a curse and possibly a danger in the finished boat. Problems here are laborious to cure later because they are almost always behind the joinery. It is important to check this work even if it has been done by the manufacturer; look at the joint all around the inside to see that the over bonding has been properly applied. All the nuts and washers must be well covered and the bonding tight up against the hull and deck, with no ragged loops hanging down.

The best moulders are Lloyd's approved. This means that their factory conditions, production methods, materials, quality, temperature control and many other factors all comply with the rigorous standards set out by Lloyds to ensure that top class work can be produced. If, in addition to these safeguards, you wish to obtain an individual moulding certificate covering your particular hull, you must inform the moulder in advance. He will then arrange for a Lloyd's surveyor to monitor the work as it progresses. This will cost more money, but will be partly reflected in the resale value.

When you have decided which hull to buy, which additional work is to be done and what extras you require, you must make arrangements with the moulder with regard to the delivery date and payment. It is standard practice throughout the boatbuilding industry that full payment is made before the hull leaves their yard. You must therefore make sure that they receive your money well in advance of the delivery.

So make your choice carefully and try not to let your enthusiasm run riot. It is obviously wiser to choose a modest boat for your first venture. Enjoy the work, complete it in a reasonable period of time and make a thoroughly good job of it, rather than do things the other way. Eventually you may wish to sell your cherished creation to build a different or larger craft. This will not be a profitable exercise if the standard of work or the quality of the materials is low.

Some people buy a hull with the object of completing it and selling at a profit as soon as it is finished. Whilst this is possible in a modest way, it is a somewhat dubious venture. This is because, although you should be able to complete a boat for less than it would cost from a builder, it is not easy to sell an amateur built boat for the price that he can command. Prospective buyers are naturally sceptical about the quality, and it can be difficult to attract them even to look at the craft once they have realised that it is not professionally built. Another reason is that as an amateur builder, you will have difficulty in buying your fittings and materials at the advantageous prices available to the professionals. This erodes much of the possible profit and you may find that the sum yielded will not compensate for the large amount of your time involved.

There are so many different types of craft available, with varying amounts of internal mouldings, joinery and detail required, that it is difficult to generalise about the number of actual man hours involved in fitting out a hull of any given size. Also, a lot depends on the time you have available, your skill, and the speed at which you work. As a guide, professional boat builders will be estimating at around 100 man hours to complete a twenty foot sailing boat with a fair amount of internal mouldings, but 1500 man hours for a thirty footer with a substantial amount of craftsman-built joinery, engine installation and electronic equipment.

2

Building
Insurance

It would be foolish to undertake any expensive or hazardous project without adequate insurance cover.

A hull sitting safely in your garden may not seem to be exposed to much risk, but you must consider transit risks, unloading accidents, fire, the possibility of the hull falling over on somebody or a tree falling on it, a lorry crashing into your garden and all kinds of possible disasters.

Transit risks are usually covered by the insurance of the vehicle which transports the hull, but you should check with the haulier that this is so and also enquire whether the upper limit of the vehicle's load cover is sufficient to cover the value of your hull. This also applies to the crane if you use one for unloading.

Most of the insurance companies dealing with private craft have special arrangements designed to cover boats under construction at home. They will require full details of the vessel including dimensions, transit cover, unloading, methods of propulsion, possible fire risks (engine fuel, gas etc) and also the values of the major units, ie hull, spars, engines etc. Do not be tempted to overestimate these because the value will be reflected in the premium. In any case, the sum payable in the event of a claim for total loss would be the company's estimation of its value, not yours.

On receipt of the details, the insurance company will quote a premium required over a given period. Quotations for insurance and the extent of the cover offered vary considerably from company to company. It is therefore advisable to obtain several quotations and then choose your company on the premium charged in relation to the cover offered and the status of the insurers.

3

The Building Site

Due account must be taken of the type of boat in relation to the proposed building site. It is no good buying a 30ft hull standing 10ft tall and hoping to fit it out over three years in the 35ft yard of a small terraced house; that would almost certainly antagonise those living nearby and possibly the local authority as well. Remember that building a boat entails you working whilst lesser mortals are trying to relax in peace. The screech of electric drills, persistent hammering and struggles with deckwork, often late at night, will not go down well with the folks next door.

Ideally, the job is best done under cover. Some people are fortunate enough to be able to rent a nearby shed or barn with electric power, from some kindly farmer. Such a building must also have adequate access for vehicles to get the hull in and, later, out again.

Most amateur builders have to make do with working in the open outside their own house, the positioning of the hull depending once again on access for lorries and cranes. When access is restricted, hulls can be lifted over houses into the working site but this entails the use of very large, expensive cranes with long reach. Extensive problems are involved with traffic, possible damage to other property, pavings, etc, so that much courage is required even to consider such a project. The weight of a boat is considerably increased by the time it is complete and this could cause even greater problems for a crane at maximum reach.

The main points to consider are: how will

the hull be unloaded on the building site? If the crane is required to get on to the site, is there room for it to operate? Is the ground firm enough to support a heavy vehicle? Discuss these questions with the transport contractor and make your decisions accordingly, well in advance of making final delivery arrangements.

If the ground is soft you will need a plentiful supply of thick boards to support vehicles as they move, or they will become stuck. Failure to provide proper support will mean aggravating delays, and further equipment or a tractor to pull them out. Costs and tempers will rise together.

Preparing the ground

Sailing boats with deep keels are laborious to fit out if their keels are standing at ground level. During the course of building you will travel hundreds of times to and from your workshop carrying tools, fittings and materials. If the journeys are made via ladders or steps up the side of the hull standing high above the ground, much time and energy will be wasted. Boats are also very much more obtrusive standing at ground level in small gardens.

If the keel is an integral part of the hull, the problem can be alleviated by standing it in a trench. Your lawn is going to get spoiled anyway and the effort of digging the trench is well worthwhile. The required length and breadth can be found by scaling from the drawing of

the boat or by measurements from a similar hull. The depth should be such that with heavy timber support blocks at the bottom, only the keel is in the hole, leaving the underbody of the hull above ground.

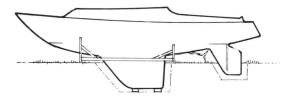

Fig 2 *Setting the hull in a trench to make access easier during building.*

If your boat has a bolt-on keel, it can be delivered in two parts, thus enabling the hull to stand at low level. The keel can then be fitted with the aid of a crane when all the other work is complete.

If a spade type rudder or propeller shaft are to be fitted before the hull is delivered, holes in the site will obviously be required in the appropriate places to accommodate these. Alternatively, the height of the hull above ground, when the keel is in a trench, must give sufficient clearance to enable the prop shaft assembly, transducers, log spinners and other underwater fittings to be fitted. It is not possible, under these circumstances, to fit a spade rudder easily without digging a very deep hole in order to get the rudder shaft up through the hull.

4
Cradles

The cradle to support the hull during the fitting out may be one which will be kept for winter storage of the finished boat. This will probably mean fairly heavy outlay before work actually starts. The other disadvantage is that the hull will be higher off the ground than is desirable and involves extra effort, as mentioned previously. These winter storage cradles, for use at the club or boatyard, are usually made to order by small

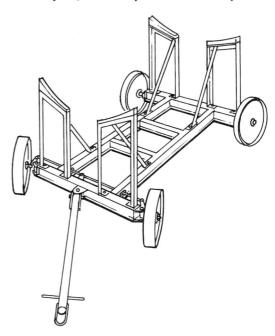

Fig 3 *A typical custom-built winter storage cradle made of steel joists and angle, fitted with wheels and steering gear from a concrete mixer.*

local engineering companies from a conglomerate of secondhand materials.

Most amateur builders will prefer to prefabricate a temporary building cradle from secondhand timber. In order to construct one in advance, measurements will have to be obtained from a similar one or from a hull at the moulder's works. Whichever source is used, the cradle must accept the hull immediately it is unloaded at your site, because there is not likely to be much time to make extensive alterations on the spot. It is better to build it to allow some slack than to attempt to make it a precise fit. The slack can be packed with blocks and wedges so that the hull can be adjusted for level later.

Use fairly heavy timber, say 4in × 2in section (old roof rafters are ideal) and fasten the end frame members with $\frac{1}{2}$in diameter bolts. These end frames should be constructed so that they are diagonally braced and are therefore integrally rigid. They can be fastened together at the appropriate distance by longitudinal timbers, as shown, using 4in nails and also fitted with diagonal struts to ensure rigidity in this direction. For boats at ground level, cross bars should be fitted to support the keel just clear of the ground. This will assist the work of painting the keel later. Boats with keel profiles that do not run parallel with the designed or load waterline (DWL or LWL) will need a cradle constructed to accommodate the keel at the correct angle, so that when the hull is in place the waterline will be horizontal. Whichever type of

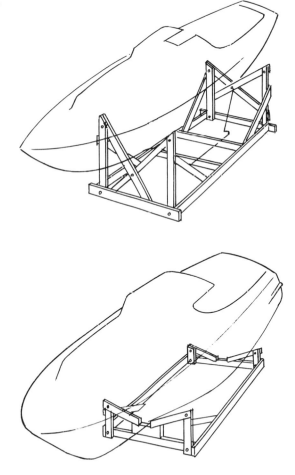

Fig 4 *Cheap timber cradles to support the hull during building or transporting.*

support is used, the bilges must not bear heavily on it, otherwise distortion and gel-coat cracking can occur. The weight must be taken on the keel alone and the cradle used merely to keep the hull in the upright position.

When the completed cradle is placed on the building site, it should be roughly levelled up in both the longitudinal and transverse planes so that, when the boat is lowered into it, only minimal adjustments will be required in order to level the hull accurately and bring the DWL horizontal. The same general remarks apply to a 'low level' cradle for a sailing boat hull with the keel in a trench, as suggested in the chapter on the building site.

The main thing is to have everything ready for the delivery so that there will be no delay: delays cost money–your money.

5

Transport and Unloading

There are three main criteria involved in choosing your transport: access for heavy vehicles to the building site, unloading facilities available on the site, and cost. You must decide how the hull is to be supported on the transport. This could be a cradle hired or borrowed, or one you have made yourself. Alternatively, if you engage a specialist boat transporter, his vehicle will usually be fitted with adjustable supports to suit most hulls.

Fig 5 *Large vehicles may be necessary at the site to carry and off-load the hull, so you must ensure that you have enough room.*

Some boat transport specialists carry portable lifting gantries on their lorries, and slings capable of lifting fairly heavy boats. For many amateur builders these can be the most sensible proposition. They are entirely self-contained, need no expensive hired cranes and are often driven by their owners. Also, the overall cost of the transport and unloading package may well be less than that of delivery on a low loader needing the help of a crane.

If a vehicle without lifting gear is to deliver the hull, a mobile crane will be required. In this case you must ensure that both can operate at the site. Discussions must take place with the delivery team and the crane owners well in advance, to anticipate any problems that may occur and avoid expensive misunderstandings and delays on delivery day. In particular, the relative times of arrival of the low loader and crane should be carefully worked out.

If unloading with a hired crane, you may also have to provide the actual lifting tackle, comprising suitable slings ready to be hooked on without delay. Boat slings are usually made from heavy duty nylon webbing about 4in wide by 30ft long or from the same length of heavy but soft laid rope, about 2in diameter, stitched in a canvas covering to prevent it from scuffing the hull. Each sling has a large eye at each end for hooking on to a crane. They are used in pairs, one around each end of the hull in conjunction with a pair of stout spreaders; these are pieces of wood about 4in × 2in section with a vee notch cut in each end. The length of spreader must be slightly greater than the width of the boat at the point where the sling is positioned. When they are fitted between the upper parts of each sling, the spreaders prevent the hull from being crushed by the slings as it is lifted. You may be able to borrow or hire

these items, but it is most unlikely that they will be provided with a hired crane or lorry unless specifically arranged.

Another way to deal with the transport problem is to despatch your winter storage cradle to the hull supplier as described earlier. Some moulders have low loader transporters from which the rear wheels can be removed and replaced by ramps. This means that the hull can be lifted into your wheeled cradle at the moulder's works and sent to you on the low loader. Unloading down the rear ramps then becomes a relatively simple task. However, you will not be able to move such a cradle on anything other than hard level surfaces without the aid of a tractor or powerful winches. Off the road, cars are rarely any use in shifting such a weight, because their clutches are unable to cope with such a heavy static pull.

If the delivery and unloading process is likely to cause a major obstruction on a public road, you must inform your local police, who can then decide whether they wish to come along on the day to take charge of traffic control; another of their concerns will be that local bus services are not disrupted. So, if your building site is on a bus route, you may have to organise the operation between bus times. It is a great help to have just a couple of friends, not a big crowd, to help generally during the unloading. They may also be able to.help the police to control the traffic.

Finally a word of warning: some companies that mould hulls can be unreliable on their promised delivery dates. You will be wise to telephone them shortly before your hull is to be delivered to ensure that all is well, and state firmly that your transport, crane etc, will be operating on the agreed day, or you may find that all your careful planning has been expensively in vain.

So, when the hull has been chosen, the moulder or agent paid, site and cradle prepared, transport and lifting arranged and friends organised to help on delivery day, good luck! When it is over, the first major step is complete.

6

Levelling the Hull

When your boat is afloat at its DWL, the internal joinery should be parallel to the waterline. Therefore, to simplify marking out and fitting, it is important that the hull is accurately levelled in both longitudinal and transverse directions to bring the waterline horizontal before work begins. This will enable the bulkheads and all furniture to be marked out and fitted with the aid of a spirit level and plumb bob. There is no reliable alternative method.

Normally, both the boot-topping line and the waterline are marked on the hull during the moulding process. They will appear as thin scribed lines, matching the lines on the original plug from which the moulds were made. If the waterline is not already marked you will have to find its position by scaling from the boat's drawing and marking them in, using a wax crayon or chinagraph pencil; avoid using spirit based felt tipped pens as they are likely to stain the gel-coat. At this stage you will only need to mark the points where the waterline meets the bow, the stern and two marks, one on each side of the hull, about half way along.

The first operation is to level the hull fore and aft (longitudinally). Assuming that the waterlines are already marked all round, the levelling can be done using a spirit level and a straight parallel board. Place the spirit level on the top edge of the board and hold the board on the waterline about halfway along the boat's length. Now adjust it until the spirit level shows horizontal, and then sight across the board at the marked waterline. It is a somewhat hose with water and hold one end level with the waterline at the bow whilst he does the same at the stern; the hose will remain full if the hull is horizontal. It is an advantage if a short length of transparent hose is attached to each end to improve your view of the level.

If the hull is not horizontal it will have to be raised with wedges or jacks at the full end of the hose, then packed up with slips of timber. Check again and repeat the process until the water levels at each end of the hose correspond with the waterline. It may be possible, if time allows, to complete this part of the levelling whilst the hull is still partially suspended on the crane or gantry as it is unloaded.

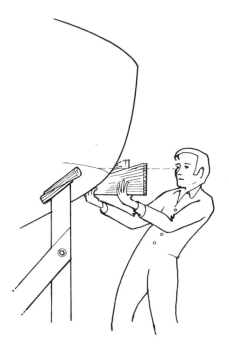

Fig 6 *Checking that the hull is level fore and aft using a spirit level, sighting the scribed waterline.*

crude method but you will be able to see whether the waterline is parallel with the board, therefore horizontal or not. Although not particularly accurate, carried out with some care this system will be good enough to achieve the desired result.

A more reliable method, which can also be applied if the waterline has not been pre-marked, is to use a length of garden hose, somewhat longer than the hull. With an assistant, fill the

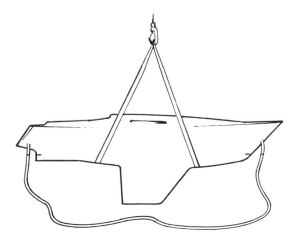

Fig 7 *A more reliable method of levelling using a water-filled hose. Levelling fore and aft is best done whilst the crane is still on site.*

The same technique can be used to level the hull transversely; this is best done at the point of maximum beam. Your reference marks can be either at the waterline or the top edge of the hull. Alternatively, using the spirit level method, you will need to select some suitable reference points on the deck moulding, such as the tops of the cockpit coamings or the decks themselves. A parallel board, placed on edge across the cockpit coamings with the spirit level placed on the top edge should be accurate enough; the board should be on edge to guard against sag. If for some reason this is not possible, an identical spacer can be placed on each deck giving sufficient height for the board to clear the superstructure; two blocks of wood,

two paint tins, any two articles the same height can be used. You ought to be able to tilt the hull transversely in its cradle easily by adjusting the bilge wedges, as there should be sufficient slack either side to allow for this.

When the hull is horizontal, lightly tap soft-wood wedges in between the hull and each of the cradle frames. Care must be taken not to hammer too hard, causing local distortion of the hull or damage to the gel-coat surface. At this stage, check again the transverse level, and when all is well, tap the wedges in equally a little tighter. Construction work in the hull, high winds and other factors can cause some movement, so skew nail the wedges to the end frames of the cradle.

If the base is on soft ground, such as your lawn or vegetable patch, it will settle after a while, so it is advisable to check the level after a few weeks, particularly after rain, and readjust if necessary.

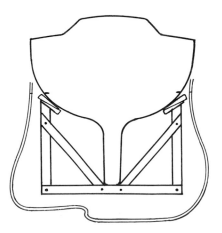

Fig 8 *Levelling the hull athwartships can be done with either the water-filled hose or a board and spirit level placed across the cockpit coamings.*

7
Facilities

Access

In order to make access to the hull easy and thus safely speed up the fitting out work, a strong flight of steps constructed from second-hand timber is a valuable asset; these can be topped by a platform at deck level. This will greatly facilitate working on board which involves many journeys to and from your workshop. If you have a plentiful supply of scrap timber or scaffolding and are fortunate enough to have a secure building site with adequate space, it is an advantage to make a platform large enough to accommodate a small bench and vice.

Covers

Most amateur builders will take considerably more than a year to complete their vessel. To improve working conditions on board during the winter months, a cover over all or part of the vessel will be required. The cover is best made from heavy gauge polythene sheeting, stretched over a wooden framework and attached by nailed battens (see fig 9), though for this type of cover, a reasonably sheltered building site is necessary. Wide polythene sheeting is usually available at most builder's merchants. To limit the size of the structure, it is only really necessary to cover the open part of the boat, because the work can be organised so that all exterior jobs are done in the open during good weather. Make the framework with a reasonably steep slope to the top, and rafters pitched at about 1ft apart; this will ensure efficient drainage of rainwater and also limit the amount of noise made by the sheeting on windy days. As you build, add diagonal struts about 2ft long at all the top corners of the main frame to stop it from racking. Then drive wooden posts, about 2in square, well into the ground close alongside each leg and nail the legs to the posts; these will act as anchors to prevent the cover from being blown over. If you can build the framework to span the steps and platform, this will in effect, create a porchway.

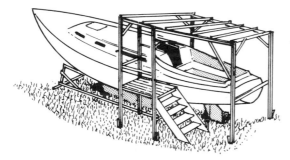

Fig 9 *Polythene sheeting fastened over a timber framework to cover at least the open part of the boat: access steps are a great advantage.*

When the framework is complete and is sufficiently rigid, cut a generous supply of battens about $1in \times \frac{1}{8}in$ section and drive 1in wire nails into them at about 6in centres. This is advisable to avoid having to fiddle about with loose nails as you are fitting the sheet.

Start by covering the ends in. It is best to carry the sheeting down the framework as far as deck level. You will probably need an assistant to hold the sheet while you nail the battens through it into the frame. Stretch the material tightly as you proceed and hammer the nails well home. Trim around the edges and then drape sheeting over the top of the frame so that it overlaps the ends and attach it in the same manner.

If your site is exposed to high winds, the cover will need to be made of tarpaulin or reinforced plastic sheeting with proper eyelet fastening points well tied down, but these are more expensive and will make the hull dark inside. However, they can be used later to cover the vessel during its annual winter lay-up.

Power and lighting

Power tools and electric lighting on board are virtually essential. In the interests of safety and convenience, run a weatherproof three-core power cable from the nearest available supply into the boat for the duration of the fitting out; the supply is best supported clear of the ground on a series of posts or along a fence. On board, there should be at least two power sockets, preferably with switches. At the other end a plug can be fitted for connection to any convenient power socket in your workshop or house. Rather than running the supply through an open window you may, for security reasons, consider drilling a hole through the window frame, passing the cable through and fitting the plug on the inside. This allows the window to be closed without interfering with the power line and the hole is easily plugged up again when no longer required. *The cable must be properly connected to earth at both ends.*

If you have room on board, it is well worth rigging a fluorescent lamp on temporary fixings at least in the main part of the boat. It is best to arrange overhead fixings for all the lighting right from the start, because wander lamps are always in the way and consequently frequently get broken. Having completed the preparation, you should now be well set to get the fitting out work started.

8

The Drawings

There is usually a minimum of three drawings supplied with a hull, showing the sailplan, deckwork and interior layout on separate sheets. If exposed to damage from resin, sawdust, grubby hands, folding or re-folding during the work, they will quickly become illegible. If you tape them to suitable pieces of hardboard they will be more convenient to work from, easier to find and will last through the whole job.

Most people are quite happy to adhere to the sailplan and deckwork drawings but, when it comes to the internal layout, some have a tendency to depart from the design. It must be realised that the space in a boat is determined not only by the deckplan but also by the section shapes. Although the hull may appear to be more than large enough for the planned accommodation, the designer has almost certainly included as much as is reasonably possible. Therefore it is best to keep to the general arrangement shown and, if you wish, make only minor alterations or add extra cupboards in odd corners.

The layout should be arranged so that an average-sized man can live on board in a modicum of comfort. This means somebody about 5ft 10in tall weighing around 160lbs, and therefore the berths, doorways, hatchways etc, must be large enough to suit such a person wearing bulky clothing or a life jacket. Even if you and your family are all on the small side, it is unwise to cut down on these sizes because your occasional guest may not appreciate it. It could also make the boat difficult to sell.

With these points in mind you will find that where possible, the headroom is usually about 6ft 2in, probably reducing forward. In some craft it is possible to gain floor space by raising the level of the cabin sole at the expense of headroom, but the temptation should be resisted for the reasons stated. Smaller craft, particularly sailing boats, will have much less than standing headroom. This is not a serious disadvantage because you will knock your head less under 4ft 9in headroom than 5ft 9in.

Similarly, berths should all be at least 6ft 2in long by 1ft 10in wide and, in the main cabin where they are also used as seats, between 1ft 2in and 1ft 6in from floor level to the top of the seat cushions. Beware of making berths too wide if you find yourself with room to spare; the sleeper will roll about too much in anything wider than 2ft 6in. Hatchways should be a minimum of 1ft 9in square with entrance doors the same width, while internal doorways can be about 1ft 6in wide. In the toilet compartment, ample shoulder room is necessary. This should be at least 2ft measured across the width of the WC. The height of the WC should be around 1ft 6in from the floor, and there should be at least 1ft 4in clear in front of the bowl when the door is shut.

The drawings are made to a specific scale, usually 1in = 1ft and although it is normally possible to scale from them they should be treated with some circumspection. For example, you must not rely on marking out your bulkhead panels solely by scaling from the drawing.

Irregularities inside the hull or slight error in the position of the bulkheads cause alteration to their shape and size.

Materials requirements can be adequately compiled from the drawings but take note of the general thickness of the plywoods, sections of solid materials etc., in order to keep the weight as low as possible commensurate with adequate strength. Some designers either expect their creations to be used stripped or they have strange ideas about the accommodation weight. This causes many boats to start off their lives floating too deep.

9

Organising the Work

The best time to take delivery of a hull is in spring or early summer. This will give you the benefit of long, light evenings and the best chance of good weather to start the deck work. It is a good plan to get as much outside work done as possible before getting too far with the interior, with the exception of the main bulkheads and the engine installation. This includes hatches, deck fittings, deck joinery, rudder fitting, propeller shaft installation and hull fittings.

If all these can be completed before winter you can work inside the hull during the cold weather with electric light, heater, tools and materials. Otherwise it will be difficult to pre-plan the work schedule accurately because bad weather can entirely disrupt it. Also in many cases, deck fittings that bolt through the deck must be fitted before the joinery to avoid problems of access later.

As the work progresses, make a list of the jobs and additional materials needed as they present themselves. The list can also include any special tools and equipment which may be required. This will help with the general planning of the work and avoid one job holding up another or being stopped by shortage of materials. Also, if you have any helpers offering their services unannounced, you will never be at a loss to direct them into a task you think they can tackle. Otherwise, when visitors arrive, greet them cordially and press on resolutely. Remember, you will be a centre of interest for 'would be' boatbuilders and they waste hours of your valuable time telling you so.

10

Materials

To be a lasting success, construction of any kind of boat must be of good quality material. The temptation to use cheaper alternatives will inevitably prove to be false economy. The whole boat, inside and out, is going to spend its life in a hostile environment of damp, cold, heat, salt water, ultra-violet light and so on, all of which are ready to attack the structure either singly or en masse. They can demolish or corrode in an astonishingly short time most of the cheaper plywoods, blockboard, chipboard, hardboard, non-waterproof glues, paints, unanodised light alloys and non-marine grades of stainless steel. So, use only the best materials even if it means that initially you have to leave off some of the bolt-on equipment or extra sails. These can always be purchased later.

Kits

Many companies now offer kits of parts for the home builder. These vary in quality and extent, possibly including glues, resins, fastenings and fittings. Just how much you buy will depend on your means, but kits are well worth consideration because through the manufacturer's ability to order in bulk, they will often represent good value and will save you much time and effort in buying your own materials. Pre-cut kits of parts for bulkheads, joinery panels etc. (often with edge trim and locker doors fitted already to go into the hull) will save hours of pre-liminary work marking out and making templates. Hull manufacturers or their agents are also often able to supply engines complete with stern gear and other complete packages, such as wiring sets, fuel tanks, instruments, spars, etc.

Plywoods

As explained in the section on bulkheads, many hulls require plain plywood bulkheads which are later faced with decorative veneered ply or vynide. The boards are most commonly available in 8ft by 4ft sheets to various thickness ranging through $\frac{1}{8}$in, $\frac{3}{16}$in, $\frac{1}{4}$in, then in $\frac{1}{8}$in steps up to $\frac{3}{4}$in. These must all be of the resin-bonded waterproof type.

When buying any plywood it is as well to examine the boards at the timber yard before actually making a purchase. Inspect the faces to check their quality, timber type and colour, finish and gaps in the veneers or any sign of delamination. The boards are commonly stocked with one finished face. This means that the opposite face may have a number of round or oval shims let into the veneer where a knot or crack has been removed. This will be of no consequence for most of the board required because at least one face will be covered later.

For the bulkheads, the most reliable are of the British Standard BS 1088 specification. They are constructed throughout with mahogany veneers and every aspect of the manufacturing process is closely controlled, but they are by far the most expensive.

A reasonably reliable alternative specification is WBP which means water boiling proof. They are made from a wide variety of timbers from mahogany to douglas fir. The American Plywood Association PS 1-74 grades A-A, A-B and B-B and the Canadian Standards Association CSA 0121 plywoods are comparable to these because the specifications demand durable timber veneers and resin bonding. The test is to boil an offcut in water for an hour, then see how the glued laminations have survived. If you can peel them apart, the board is unsuitable for marine use.

For the general faced joinery panels you may decide to use boards with a decorative veneer rather than plain board. The most popular is teak because it has a rich colour with wonderful grain patterns.

These faced boards must also be resin-bonded WBP exterior grade. (Do not accept interior grade although it is to be used inside the boat.) The body veneers are sometimes made from birch which is not particularly durable, white in colour and almost featureless. The reverse side has a mahogany balancing veneer to stabilise the board, that is, to minimise the tendency to warp caused by the teak face. This balancer also improves the appearance of the inside where visible in such places as locker doors and so on.

If you decide to use a thin ply facing on your bulkheads, these boards will not need the balancing veneer as they will be fully supported by the bulkhead and therefore cannot warp.

Hardwoods

All of the external joinery on a boat must be made from the most durable timber available within your budget. Teak is best for durability and appearance, followed closely by its relatives afrormosia and iroko. These are all extremely durable with or without paint or varnish (they are sometimes best if oiled) and so are ideal for marine use. Below decks it is particularly important to match the plywood veneered faces with cappings and trim in timber of the same species. The appearance of even the finest joinery can be ruined by mismatched timber, so never try to economise by using cheaper trim.

The price per unit of these hardwoods tends to vary considerably with the species and the sizes ordered. For example, teak in relatively short lengths (around 8ft), is approximately double the price of afrormosia but, if you specify it much longer (say 15ft) the price rises astronomically. On the other hand afrormosia, which is plain dark brown, and iroko, an insipid yellowish colour, and the various mahoganies are available economically up to about 20ft.

Make enquiries at your local timber yard to make comparisons and do not order timber in excessive lengths. If extra long items of joinery are required, such as toe rails or rubbing strakes, it is as well to buy in economical lengths and scarph joint the pieces as required rather than pay twice the price to achieve the same result.

Apart from the influence of cost, bear in mind

that teak is easy to finish with hand tools whilst afrormosia, iroko and many mahoganies are very difficult because they have twisted grain. This means that unless you buy teak, your facing timbers must be purchased with machine finished faces which add cost. Alternatively, you must have a sawbench with a sharp, tungsten carbide tipped blade, capable of producing high quality work which will only need finishing with glasspaper.

Most of the timber used in finishing a fibreglass craft is required in only small sections. However, if the design of your boat requires wide sections anywhere, perhaps cockpit coamings, you must select boards that are not likely to bow across their section. This is influenced by the part of the log from which they are cut. As can be seen in fig 10a, the most economical way of cutting is in parallel slices. These are called *through and through* boards. The ones that are cut passing through the centre of the log are stable because the growth rings run across the board at a steep angle ($45°$ and above). This means that shrinkage will be reasonably consistent in both directions. Boards cut further from the middle have growth rings running along their section in shallow arcs. This causes the boards to bow in the opposite direction to the rings.

For the same reason, boards cut in the manner known as *quarter sawn* are the most stable (see fig 10b) but this is less popular with the merchant due to the wastage involved.

The best timber in any log is in the centre. It

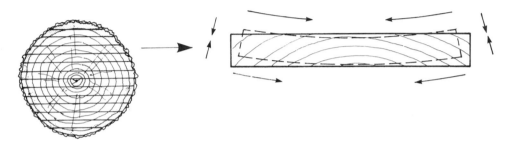

Fig 10a *The most economical, 'through and through' method of cutting a log produces a majority of boards with a tendency to warp, particularly if they are wide.*

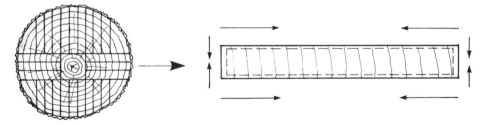

Fig 10b *Quarter sawn boards have the growth rings running at a steep angle to their faces and are therefore less inclined to warp.*

is harder and richer in colour than the outer part which is called sapwood. Sapwood is often infected with worm holes and is of poor quality so it should be rejected.

When purchasing any type of timber, you must state whether you require it *rough sawn*, *prepared* or *finished size*. As so many different sections will be required throughout the job, it will be expensive to obtain them all in planed finish, so some economies can be made, dependent on the tools available at home.

Timber is cut from logs in a range of nominal sizes, $\frac{3}{4}$in, 1in, 1$\frac{1}{4}$in thick and so on and can be purchased in this condition as *rough sawn*. This is the cheapest way to buy provided that you possess a powerful sawbench capable of cutting at least 2in deep. An electric drill with saw attachment is not adequate. However, if you do have a sawbench, timber can be purchased in larger random sections and prepared down as required, and this is particularly advantageous with teak.

Smooth planed faces are specified as *prepared*, for example *1in prepared*. This is 1in thick sawn board, planed both sides by machine which results in a thickness between $\frac{3}{4}$in to $\frac{7}{8}$in, so you must allow for this. If a specific planed size is required at exactly say 1in, you must order *1in finished size* and this will be machined from $1\frac{1}{4}$in sawn board, so will obviously cost more. It is therefore economically sensible to arrange the construction work using prepared sizes.

Other timbers

Floors, shelf supports, struts and hidden joinery pieces, are also best made from hardwood such as the cheaper mahoganies, but can for economy reasons be made from softwood of most varieties provided that it is reasonably free from knots and splits. Remember that softwoods are not as strong or durable as hardwood and are also more knot prone and inclined to more shrinkage movement. With regard to cutting, preparation and purchasing, the general rules as for hardwood apply. Where softwood is to be used in unventilated areas, it is advisable to paint it with a wood preservative after assembly to prevent the formation of fungus and rot.

Adhesives

For all marine work, external and internal, a good waterproof glue of the urea formaldehyde type is necessary. Various brands are easily obtained in hardware shops and are suitable for joining most timbers. As with most glues, they are affected by temperature, and cure much faster in warm conditions. Naturally oily timbers or structural woodwork that will be subjected to heavy strain and damp must be glued with a resorcinol adhesive but this type tends to be obtainable only direct from the manufacturers. It is possible to join teak using urea adhesives but not so reliable, particularly if the surfaces are freshly cut, so if possible leave the parts to be joined to dry out for a while before assembling.

For attaching plastic laminates, thin ply, veneer and foam-backed vinyl to wood, a contact adhesive is required, but they are not fully waterproof and are therefore not suitable for external use.

Fastenings

In a marine environment extreme care must be used in selecting fastenings to minimize the risk of inducing electrolysis which can destroy metal. Electrolysis will occur spontaneously between metals of dissimilar electrical potential when immersed in sea water which is, in effect, an electrolyte. The metals, which need not be in direct contact with each other, form the two poles of a cell similar to a car battery and rapid corrosion will take place. This can be minimised by fitting a sacrificial zinc anode to attract the current and the corrosion. Many hull fittings including valves, propeller brackets etc, are made from one of the various brass or bronze alloys. Silicon bronze or stainless steel bolts are suitable for these. *Never* use plain steel or galvanised steel bolts underwater. Due to the salt atmosphere of the marine environment, electrolytic corrosion can also occur on deck although less vigorously than underwater. Similar care is therefore needed with the selection of the deckwork fastenings.

All fastenings must have high resistance to marine corrosion wherever they are used. Generally, marine grade stainless steel machine screws, bolts, washers, nuts and wood screws should be used on deck. These are all expensive so if possible, work out the quantities of each size and type required and buy in bulk to reduce the cost. In this respect it is important to choose standard or 'preferred' sizes because the manufacturers sometimes charge up to ten times the normal price for 'non-preferred' screw sizes.

For some low stress applications on deck, such as wood toe rails and rubbing strakes where long through bolts are required, you can make savings by using hot dipped galvanised bolts (not electro-plated zinc). The toe rail should be bedded in mastic, the bolt head set in a deep counterbore and plugged so that it is well protected.

Down below, the panel pins and screws required in the woodwork may be of brass. Another useful fastening for marine work is the barbed nail made in monel metal.

Self tapping screws

These provide secure fastenings for many small fittings and pieces of trim to fibreglass. They are obtainable in a wide range of sizes, lengths and head shapes. They must, without exception, be made in stainless steel to provide the necessary corrosion resistance and high torsional strength. Fibreglass is extremely tough material and therefore some force is required to drive the screws into it. The holes into which they are to be driven must be drilled about 0·01 in larger in diameter than the screw core to avoid binding and consequent breakage. Before working on the boat itself, try out your drill size by drilling and driving a screw through a piece of scrap fibreglass. You will not want broken screws in finished work. A smear of tallow on each screw before fitting will make them drive more easily.

Mastic

All of the exterior joinery, deck fittings and hull fittings must be bedded on a good marine mastic. This is a waterproof non-hardening compound. It is to prevent water getting underneath the fittings, causing leaks by capillary action through bolt and screw holes, or rot from developing under woodwork.

It is available in tins for application with a putty knife, in soft containers similar to large toothpaste tubes, or in rigid tubes for use with a special applicator gun. This latter type is the quickest, most convenient to use and most economical, although involving the additional cost of the gun. These cost little and are worthwhile on boats requiring extensive applications of mastic, such as under toe rails etc: much time and trouble can be saved.

A better, although rather more expensive, alternative is to use a two part polysulphide synthetic bedding compound (PRC). This is supplied in tins with a small pot of catalyst compound which has to be mixed in proportion to the contents of the tin. You must mix only the quantity you require, because as soon as the catalyst is added, it begins to cure into a dry, rubber-like material.

Fibreglass materials

The size and complexity of your boat will determine the quantity and variety of materials needed for fitting all the joinery, bulkheads, engine bearers etc. The list of raw materials now available to make fibreglass and its associated fillers etc, is fairly extensive but basically you will need fibreglass chopped strand mat (CSM), resin, accelerator, catalyst, gel-coat, resin putty and acetone.

These can usually be purchased at the outset of the project from the hull manufacturer, whose advice can be sought with regard to the quantities and types required. This will of course, be affected not only by the size of your

vessel but also the amount of work left to be done. If you do not purchase your materials from the moulder you must check that their type is compatible with those used in the hull. As a rough guide, a small boat of about 20ft with hull, deck and bulkheads fitted and bonded will require only about five gallons of resin and three pounds of resin putty, whilst a 30ft boat with no preliminary work done could need twenty-five to thirty gallons of resin.

Having worked out how much you need, you must also consider the probable duration of the work and the rate at which the resin and other materials are likely to be used because they have a shelf-life of only about six months when stored in cool, dry conditions. It may therefore be provident to purchase a limited quantity to start with. There are several reputable companies that advertise these materials regularly and will supply an excellent catalogue which not only lists and prices the items but also explains in lucid terms the manufacturing techniques involved.

If you have no experience whatever of fibreglass work you would be wise to seek a good book on the subject (*Fibreglass Boats* by Hugo du Plessis is comprehensive) or, better still, find somebody to show you the techniques initially by perhaps bonding some scrap pieces of timber together. The chopped strand mats used for bonding the various parts into a boat are either $1\frac{1}{2}$ or 2oz mat. The material is usually supplied in rolls $1\frac{1}{2}$yds wide and you will need between 5yds and 30yds depending again on how much

work there will be to tackle. Fillers can be
added to resin or resin putties used to form
solid bedding areas where required under certain
fittings such as 'A' brackets and the like. Gel–
coat of the colour to match your hull or deck is
mixed in a similar manner to ordinary resin
and is used for filling screw holes or damaged
corners of the mouldings.

Setting Out

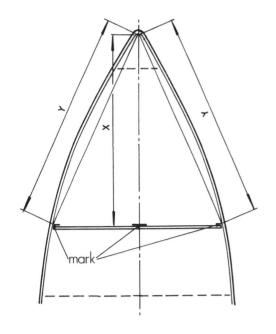

Fig 11 *Setting out the position for the first bulkhead which will be the datum for the entire accommodation layout.*

The first job to be tackled inside the hull is to set out the position of the main transverse bulkhead, which will be the datum for the other bulkheads. This will be the key to the correct siting of the entire accommodation and any error in its position can have a cumulative effect. A few inches may make the difference as to whether the galley stove will go in, or whether there is enough room at the chart table. In sailing boats, the position of the bulkhead in the area of the mast is often of further structural significance but we will consider this point later.

Select a bulkhead somewhere around the mid part of the accommodation as your datum; in a small sailing boat, this will almost certainly be the main bulkhead under the mast. If the accommodation in a larger boat, either power or sail, is of the style with double bulkheads in this area, then the datum should be the forward one of the two.

As the hull has been set up with the waterline horizontal, only three marks will be necessary to erect the datum bulkhead. From the drawings, measure with a scale rule the dimension from the inside of the bow to the forward face of the datum. Using a wax crayon mark this position (see fig 11, dimension x) on the inside of the deck moulding. Then measure the diagonal (see fig 11, dimension y) from the drawing and mark these on the inside of the hull each side at about 6in below the deck.

When this bulkhead has been set up correctly and bonded to the hull, all the other joinery work can be measured from it.

The Bulkheads

In some designs, it is necessary to have the bulkheads installed by the supplier before the deck is fitted. This can be for several reasons:

1 Difficulty of getting large panels into the hull
2 Hull requires stiffening before ejection from the mould
3 Bulkheads must be fitted in conjunction with head linings

In these cases this chapter will not apply but for most of the smaller or cheaper hulls now available, mostly without fibreglass headlinings, bulkheads are not normally fitted by the supplier.

Assuming your hull has no bulkheads fitted, taking the datum bulkhead first, make a template of one half of the curve where it touches the hull from the inside of the hull itself. This template will be used to mark out the plywood bulkhead panels. The template can be conveniently made up in sections from any available materials such as hardboard or plywood offcuts etc, and then attached to each other in situ. Cut each piece roughly to shape and offer it to the hull in vertical line with its position marks. Trim the template until you achieve a reasonable fit and, when satisfactory, carry on progressively around the one half of the hull with further pieces of board cut to overlap as shown (see fig 12). The template does not need to be an accurate fit to the hull and where it passes over stringers etc, can be cut to give some clearance.

When the half template is complete, ensure

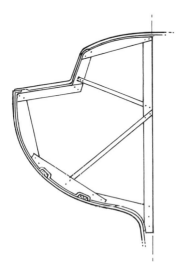

Fig 12 *Templates of each bulkhead can be made from pieces of scrap timber, ply or hardboard, nailed and braced diagonally.*

that it will not distort in profile by attaching plenty of cross stiffening pieces and mark the hull centreline positions at the top and bottom as shown. The opposite side of the hull is, of course, a duplicate of the reverse side of the template.

In order to get the bulkhead panels into the hull, you will need to ascertain by measurement the largest width that can be passed through the main hatchway. Some designs have a long cabin window at each side and these are large enough to allow a complete half bulkhead through. Otherwise you have to build up from smaller sections.

Having established the largest width that can be passed into the hull, the template can now be used to mark out the plywood panels. Assuming that the complete half bulkhead will pass into the hull, lay the template on to the plywood sheet, with the top and bottom centreline marks in line with one edge, and draw around with a pencil. Cut around the profile with a jigsaw and trim the straight edge of the panel with a plane ready to achieve a good butt joint with the opposite half. If the bulkhead has to be divided into smaller sections, adjust your marking out accordingly.

Deal with the opposite half in the same way and lay out the two halves to check for a good, tight butt joint. From the drawing, lightly mark out the position of the doorway and cut it out, smaller by about 1in all round. This is so that the doorway can be accurately marked out and re-cut after the bulkhead has been erected and bonded into the hull.

Consult the drawing to see what size fibreglass flanges are recommended around the bulkhead (3in to 4in is about the norm). Mark a line this distance in from the edge of the bulkheads both sides of both halves (not along the butt edge) indicating the flange length and cross score deeply outside this line with the corner of an old chisel to form a key for the flanges.

Finally, before taking the panels into the hull, cut and fit a temporary butt strap at both the top and bottom of the join in the area of the cross scoring. Then remove the butt straps and take the panels into the hull.

The main problem to be overcome in erecting the larger bulkheads is that of holding them in position whilst they are tacked to the hull with fibreglass. There are several ways of tackling the problem and the choice will depend on the shape of the hull. Probably the most universal method is to fit both parts together, as this simplifies the holding problem.

With an assistant, offer the two parts of the bulkhead up to their approximate positions individually. They should go easily into place with no pressure on the hull. In fact, it is desirable

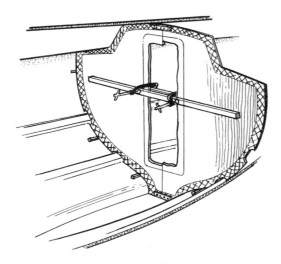

Fig. 13 *The two halves of a bulkhead, joined together temporarily with ply butt straps and held around the hull with wedges ready for the initial tack bondings. Alignment of the two halves is ensured by two boards clamped across the faces.*

that they have some clearance, to avoid local stressing which can cause gel-coat cracks on the outside later on. Position the two halves into line with each other in their approximate location in the hull, re-fit the butt straps and clamp two pieces of timber, one each side as shown, to align the two halves. The whole bulkhead assembly can be eased up to the position marks under the deck moulding and on the hull, and checked vertically with a spirit level. When all is satisfactorily in position, lightly tap a few softwood wedges between it and the hull in strategic places.

The bulkhead assembly is now ready to be bonded to the hull, though unless you are an experienced and clean worker of polyester resin, it is not wise to attempt the job without masking the bulkhead first. To do this, all you need is to hang sheets of newspaper over both faces and attach them with tape, running the tape around the edge of the newspapers leaving the cross-scored area exposed.

Initially, the bulkhead should be tack bonded to the hull in several positions around its perimeter so that it is rigidly held in place whilst the wedges and any other temporary supports are removed, to clear the way to the full bonding. With a number of short pieces of chopped strand mat (CSM) about 6in square, tack bond the bulkhead to the hull at intervals around the bulkhead on both sides. When the resin is cured, remove all the wedges and temporary supports.

The bulkhead can now be fully bonded in position with built up flanges in accordance

Fig 14 *Masking the bulkhead faces and beginning to make the bond.*

with the designer's recommendations regarding the number and weight of the laminates. The newspaper mask should be removed whilst the resin is still tacky by running a sharp knife around the outer edge of the tape and peeling the whole mask away.

All the other bulkheads can now be positioned in relation to the datum as shown on the drawing.

Mark the appropriate distance on each side of the hull in order to ensure that everything is parallel.

Half bulkheads

Generally these can be treated in the same way as the other bulkheads except that, as they do not pass continuously right across the hull, other methods of holding them in position whilst they are bonded must be employed.

Cut a beam to fit across the hull in position

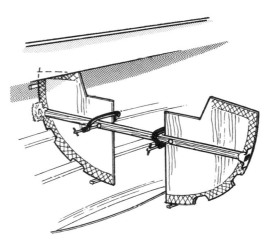

Fig 15 *Setting up half bulkheads. Note the temporary beam bonded in position across the hull.*

across one face of the bulkhead near the top (see fig 15). Bond the beam into position temporarily with fibreglass flanges, only one mat thick on each side. This will hold the beam quite rigidly enough to support the half bulkheads. Clamp the halves in position against the beam as shown, check they are vertical, and wedge where necessary to obtain control all round and tack bond to the hull as previously described.

When the tack bondings have cured, remove all the clamps, cut the flanges holding the beam and remove it. Then bond fully around the bulk-heads both sides in the normal way. This method will ensure that the halves are accurately positioned and are in line with each other.

In many instances it is not possible to conceal the fibreglass bulkhead flanges fully behind the other joinery so it is best to use plain, un-faced ply for the bulkheads themselves. When they are fully bonded into the hull they can then be faced with thin ply, vynide or laminated plastic, covering the complete bulkhead and its flanges. This will be dealt with in chapter 23.

13
Bonding with Fibreglass

The bulkheads and major items of joinery are bonded to the inside of the hull with strips of fibreglass chopped strand mat cut into lengths of about 24in to 36in for ease of handling.

For the main bulkheads, particularly in the area of the mast in a sailing boat, these flanges are required to cope with a considerable strain so it is most important that they are correctly constructed. The flange size and the number of mats is sometimes specified on the drawings but if not, as a general guide, they should be about 4in wide by 3 mats thick around the main bulkheads of a 20ft boat to 5in by 4 mats thick on a

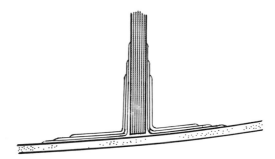

Fig 16   *A typical bonded flange built up with strips of 2 oz chopped strand mat.*

30ft sailing boat. It is advisable to step successive layers of CSM back as shown (see fig 16) in order to taper the flanges.

After the bulkheads have been set up and masked with tape and newspaper ready for bonding, cut up sufficient strips of CSM to complete the bond and stack them adjacent to the bulkhead in their various widths ready for application. For a 4in flange, the strips would be 8in × 24in stepping down to say 6in × 24in and 4in × 24in. When you are ready to start, mix the resin as described and begin the bonding, working around the bulkhead. The successive layers of glass mats can be applied directly without waiting for the resin to cure. The joints in the strips should not coincide in adjacent layers, but be overlapped rather as bricks in a wall.

Mixing and applying the resin

Working with polyester resin is a messy business, particularly if you are inexperienced. The ingredients are all potential skin irritants so use a good barrier cream and avoid contamination of the skin, because as you work the resin will start to cure on your hands. In addition, the fibreglass will tend to attach itself to you as you lay successive strips and the resultant mess is most troublesome to remove, particularly from the fingernails. This can be controlled to some extent by wiping your hands occasionally with acetone or by wearing a cheap pair of domestic rubber gloves.

After a bonding session, if your hands are contaminated, wash them in acetone, then in hot water and strong detergent, dry and apply skin cream.

WARNING: Polyester resins and acetone are highly flammable and give off toxic fumes.

Therefore, good ventilation in the work area is essential and no one should smoke near these materials.

In order to start curing or setting the resin, two additional components are required to be mixed into it. These are accelerator (a cobalt naphanate in styrene) and hardener or catalyst (methyl ethyl ketone peroxide). Most resins are now supplied pre-accelerated which means that no further accelerator is required and only hardener is required to start the cure. It is therefore important to check when you purchase it whether the accelerator has been included or not. Accelerator and catalyst must never be allowed to be in direct contact with each other as an explosion is possible. These materials are now supplied in metric quantities.

The ratio of accelerator to catalyst is 1 to 1 in approximately 100 of resin (ie 1% each) which is equivalent to adding 10gm of each to 1kilo of resin. This should give the relatively slow setting period of about half an hour, but in cool conditions, or if you require a faster set, increase the ratio to about 2%. The minimum curing temperature is about 60°F (16°C). The quantities of accelerator and catalyst in each mix must be carefully controlled, so a couple of small measuring cylinders will be required.

If your resin is unaccelerated (colourless), you must, for each mix, add the accelerator in the correct quantity first, and stir it in well; then add the catalyst, stir and start bonding immediately. If it is pre-accelerated (pinkish colour), only the catalyst will have to be added.

Using a small container such as a cheap plastic bowl, mix about $\frac{1}{2}$kg (1lb) at first, adding sufficient accelerator and catalyst to achieve a slow set. This will enable you to get used to applying it without the set starting before you have used all that you have mixed. If you do not work quickly enough, the resin will begin to set or gel in the bowl and become impossible to work. As you become more skilled you may be able to make faster mixes with advantage. Do not however, make the mix too slow or it will run out of the CSM bondings before it begins to set causing them to be resin shy and hence weak.

You will need a cheap 2in paint brush or a special laminating roller to impregnate the glass mats with the resin. With the resin mixed, brush a generous coat over the area of bulkhead and hull to be covered by the first strip of CSM and lay the strip in place. The CSM will at first be somewhat resistant to taking the exact shape required, but carry straight on by stippling another generous coat of resin through its entire surface. Now carry on quickly in the same manner with the adjoining strip of CSM overlapping it by about 1in. This will give the first piece time to impregnate fully or wet-out. You can see when this is complete by the change in colour of the CSM from white to an even grey.

Carry on in this manner, working one strip ahead, all around the bulkhead. If you work quickly and efficiently, you will be able to carry on mixing and using the resin continuously, leaving the cleaning of the brush, bowl and your hands until you are finished. Otherwise you may have to rinse out the brush and bowl occasionally with a little acetone. When the first layer is complete, carry on immediately with the second and so on, building up the flange required before any of the resin is fully cured. This ensures a good chemical bond between layers.

When you have completed the bond, pour a small quantity of acetone into your mixing bowl and with the brush, thoroughly clean the bowl and your hands. Then repeat the process using hot water and strong detergent solution, working the bristles of the brush vigorously to wash the resin out. Watch the resin begin to cure and when it becomes tacky or semi-hard, run a sharp knife around the outer edge of the masking tape and peel away the mask. If you leave this job until the resin has cured, it will take you ten times as long.

Although the resin sets fairly quickly, it will take about a week to cure fully, so any subsequent grinding or drilling required should be delayed until then.

14

Engine Selection

Petrol (gasolene) or diesel? The choice is yours, but if you have no pre-conceived ideas about which it is to be, the fundamental points for and against each are as follows:

	For	Against
Lighter weight per HP	Petrol	Diesel
Quieter	Petrol	Diesel
Cheaper initial cost	Petrol	Diesel
More economical	Diesel	Petrol
Less flammable fuel	Diesel	Petrol
Less essential electrics	Diesel	Petrol
Less vibration	Petrol	Diesel
Greater reliability	Diesel	Petrol
Less smell	Petrol	Diesel
Less toxic exhaust	Diesel	Petrol

They appear to be fairly evenly matched on the chart but it does show some individually decisive points in favour of diesels such as economy, reliability, absence of essential and vulnerable electrics (ignition circuit) and much less fire risk.

The size, make and model of the recommended engine will normally be shown on the drawings. The designer will have selected this to suit the characteristics and requirements of the boat. For a power boat, the main criteria is to provide just sufficient power to give maximum hull speed, taking into account the extra power required to cope with headwinds and rough water conditions.

This maximum speed for any hull is approximately $1 \cdot 4 \times \sqrt[2]{\text{waterline length in ft}} = $ speed in knots. This means that for a hull with a waterline length of 25ft the maximum theoretical speed *whatever engine or sail power is applied* is only about 7 knots whilst the hull is *floating*. To exceed this speed, the hull must plane. Therefore, if the hull is the wrong shape for planing, any extra power applied will be wasted in creating a larger wave system which is dragged along with the boat.

Boats designed to plane on the surface generally have hulls of flat vee section underwater and their construction is kept as light as possible. Engines for these craft can justifiably be much more powerful in order to achieve the desired planing speed, commensurate with engine size and weight.

Sailing craft have different requirements because their engines are needed only as auxiliaries, the main power being provided by the sails. The need to minimise the weight and the space occupied by the engine, plus the desire to keep the propeller small, dictates that a relatively small, low powered engine is fitted. When deciding which unit to fit, many people fail to realise that a large auxiliary engine means unnecessary weight, problems with the accommodation and a large propeller which is a tremendous drag on the boat's speed under sail.

15

Engine Installation

The prospect of making a complete inboard engine installation in a boat is daunting for many amateur craftsmen. However, like any other job it is possible to break the work down into a series of planned, logical steps once the concept is understood.

The crucial point is that the propeller shaft should be installed at the correct angle (as shown in the design) within the hull, should lie true in its bearings and be in accurate alignment with the centreline of the output flange on the engine or gearbox. The principle is the same whether the engine is a little 4 hp auxiliary for a sailing boat or a 100 hp power boat engine.

The main problem for the amateur, working at home without heavy lifting tackle on hand, is hoisting the engine into the hull. Whether you can solve this problem decides whether you have the engine fitted professionally or tackle the job yourself. If you take delivery of the hull with the deck and superstructure fitted, you must make certain in advance that the engine will pass either through the main hatchway or through a cockpit floor hatch. You may be able to arrange with the hull manufacturer to have the engine lifted into the hull before he fits the deck and superstructure. In this case the engine can be temporarily tacked down in its pallet with fibreglass anywhere in the middle section of the hull to prevent it moving during transportation. It will then be possible to move the engine using blocks of timber, levers and muscle power, after you have fitted the bearers.

When planning the installation work, try to

anticipate the problems peculiar to your hull. For example, if the fuel tank is to be sited aft of the engine, it will be difficult in most boats to get it in after the engine has been fitted, so work out carefully what is to be the sequence of operations. It is always wise to consult the engine manufacturer's pamphlets or handbook before starting work. Some handbooks have chapters devoted entirely to installation, whilst other manufacturers publish separate instructions for installers.

Some amateur builders, for economy reasons, fit car or van engines into boats of various types. This should never be done until the engine has been properly marinised by a specialist, because apart from the work of conversion, in their standard form, the engine, gear box and many other features are totally unsuitable for marine use. See *Marine Conversions* by Nigel Warren (Adlard Coles Ltd).

There are five main types of engine installation available for small craft. They are (a) traditional in-line (b) 'V' drive (c) 'Z' drive (d) hydraulic and (e) 'S' drive. The traditional in-line installation is common to boats and ships of all shapes and sizes, and is the most straightforward to deal with, so this will be the one detailed in this book. 'V' drive and 'Z' drives are used almost exclusively to power boats in order to maximise the amount of space for accommodation in the middle part of the hull, whereas hydraulic drives enable the engine to be fitted amidships in a racing yacht to keep the weight away from the ends. The 'S' drive,

recently introduced as a package unit complete with propeller, mounting flange and engine bed for use as a sailing boat auxiliary, has the advantage of being simple to fit. The general principles employed on the traditional in-line installation are, however, largely relevant to the other four.

Most designers specify on the drawings the engine which they consider most suitable for the boat. Any departure from the specified engine should not be made without careful comparisons and consideration of weight, installation angle and engine and propeller size. It is best to consult an expert if you wish to make modifications to the specification. If you are installing the engine specified and shown on the drawing, you will be able to see the intended position of the assembly, and start setting up by scaling measurements off the drawing. If it is not shown or a different one is to be fitted, the engine and propeller assembly must be drawn in accurately to scale, using the manufacturer's outline drawing, to enable the setting up dimensions to be determined.

Marine engines are traditionally mounted rigidly on their beds and connected directly to a propeller shaft which runs through a fixed inboard gland. In modern pleasure craft, the practice of fitting the engine on special resilient mounting blocks is becoming more popular. This helps to reduce vibration and noise, but also requires a flexible inboard gland fitting and possibly a flexible shaft coupling as well, in order to accommodate the engine movement. How-

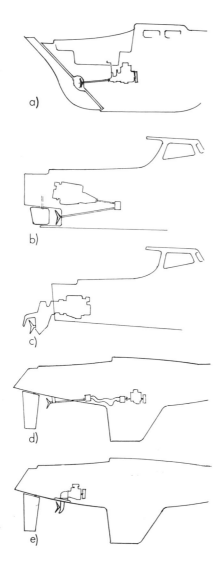

ever, it is still important that the axial alignment of the assembly is correct, and so allowance must be made for these items when setting
up. You must check that the drawing shows
the specific model to be fitted, whether it has a
reduction gearbox or not, and so on, because
handbooks can refer to the whole range of
engines with various equipment attached.

First construct a jig form of the engine base
(see figs 18 and 19). This jig made from scrap
timber should be a replica as regards the fixing
bolt holes and the centre line of the output
flange. The dimensions for the jig can be taken
from either the manufacturer's drawing or direct
from the engine itself. It is advisable to duplicate
on the bottom of the jig such features as the
sump and flywheel, that project below the feet
of the engine. This will ensure that you have
sufficient clearance between the beds.

Now for the setting up. Normally, the datum
point for any installation is the shaft centreline
immediately in front of the propeller.

Boats with propeller skegs

Boats which have a single centreline-mounted
engine with the shaft passing outboard through
a propeller skeg normally have an enlarged
boss at this point, so there will be no problem

*Fig 17   Five types of engine installation a) traditional
in line b) 'V' drive c) 'Z' drive d) hydraulic e) inboard
'Z' drive*

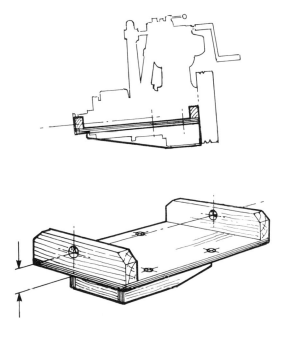

Figs 18 and 19   *A wooden replica of the engine base to facilitate the initial alignment of the propeller shaft assembly and engine bed.*

in finding this datum. Drill a small pilot hole through the centre of the boss as a guide for opening out the hole. Then, after making a general check both inside and outside that the position is correct, enlarge the hole using a tank cutter to suit the diameter of the outboard bearing spigot. The hull should be at

least ¾in thick at this point so the outboard bearing can be fitted dry and the two fixing holes positioned and tapped through for machine screws. Screw in the two screws temporarily. These should be of either stainless steel or silicon bronze. The face of the boss behind the bearing may need trimming to ensure correct alignment of the assembly later.

Now screw the stern tube and inboard gland assembly loosely into the outboard fitting from the inside of the hull. The gland fitting itself will have two holes through its flange, similar to the outboard bearing and these must be bolted to a web or low bulkhead glassed into the hull as shown in fig 20.

There are two methods that can be used for setting up the alignment. The easiest is to use a long piece of ground steel rod the same diameter as your shaft. This rod must be at least equal in length to the distance from the front end of the engine to the aft face of the outboard bearing. The idea is to set the rod up inside the hull so that it lies accurately on the proposed centreline of the engine and shaft assembly. This will be the datum from which the stern gear and the engine bed is installed. You may be able to borrow a length of suitable material from a local engineering company.

From the inside of the hull, push the rod through the outboard bearing until the end just emerges on the outside. Keeping the inboard end of the rod well supported to avoid wrenching the bearing off, set up a datum support just forward of the proposed engine position. The

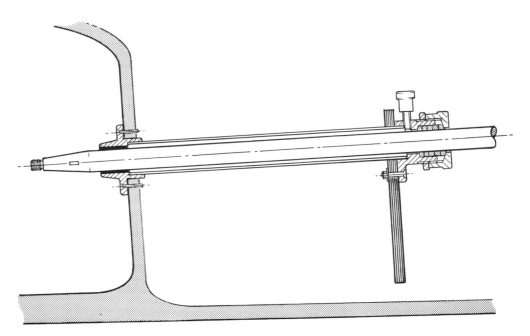

Fig 20 *Traditional stern tube and propeller shaft assembly fitted through the skeg.*

height of the support will be determined from a line projected through the engine centreline on the drawing. If you have a bulkhead around this area it will be convenient to attach the support to that.

The other method is to use a piano wire instead of a rod. The principle is the same except that the outer end must be fitted accurately through the centre of a tapered plug inserted from the outside of the outboard bearing and the forward end tensioned up to the temporary support.

With the outboard bearing bolts loose, set up the stern tube assembly in alignment with the rod or wire and check on the outside of the hull to ensure that the outboard bearing flange is lying flat on the face of the hull boss. It is unlikely to be accurate initially. If the error is small, it can be corrected by skimming the boss face with a tungsten carbide disc. For a larger correction you will have to rough back the hull gel-coat and build up a suitable pad with resin filler. The stern gear assembly can then be re-fitted and aligned whilst the pad is still wet.

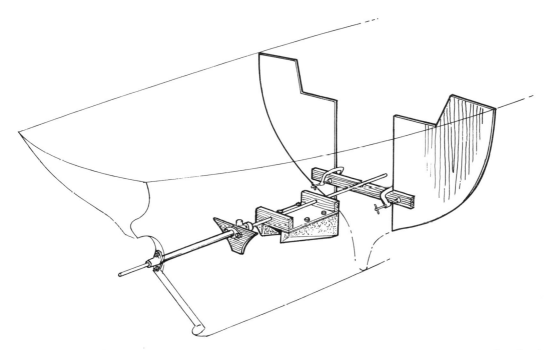

Fig 21   *Aligning the engine bed with the stern tube assembly, using the engine template and a length of steel rod.*

Leave the surplus filler to cure for trimming later.

When the alignment is satisfactory, make a cardboard template of the shape of the web to which the inboard gland fitting will be bolted. This web, which can be made from either plywood or fibreglass at least ½in thick, need not fit the hull accurately because the subsequent resin bonding will take care of all the irregularities. Slip the web over the stern tube, screw the

inboard gland fitting on to the tube, bolt its flange to the web and refit the assembly, keeping a check on the alignment as the work progresses.

Now the engine jig can be fitted on to the rod and, keeping the assembly supported the whole time, slide it down until it reaches the correct position. Level it transversely and support its weight on blocks to prevent it from distorting the alignment rod. With the engine jig satisfactorily set up, make a template for the beds. As each side should be identical, only one template will be necessary. If the engine is to be installed on resilient mounts, the depth of the mounts must be deducted from the height of the beds.

Remember that if the hull has much shape to it in this area, the beds will be deeper towards the centreline of the hull so some allowance should be made for this when making them.

Boats without propeller skegs

Many modern light displacement sailing craft, and also power craft with two engines, do not have propeller skegs. In these cases, the outboard shaft bearing will be carried on either an 'A' or 'P' bracket. Probably the most common type of 'P' bracket for modern craft is the plain shank type which is fitted through the hull. This has the advantage of being suitable for virtually all craft without skegs.

Mark the position for the 'P' bracket on the hull and cut a slot through to suit the shank. This slot should be bevelled on the inside to encourage the subsequent fibreglass bonding to grip the shank at the hull joint. Insert the 'P' bracket into the hull and set it up to the drawing position. Inside the hull the bracket is usually attached by bolted lugs to a plywood web fitted and bonded to the hull so you can cut a cardboard template for this, adjacent to the bracket inside. Cut the web from plywood at least $\frac{1}{2}$in thick and bolt the 'P' bracket to it

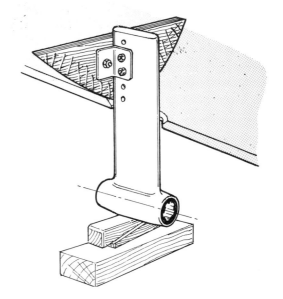

Fig 22 *Setting the 'P' bracket in the hull ready to be aligned with the shaft, tube and inboard bearing.*

as shown leaving the assembly loose in the hull for alignment later.

If the bracket has hull flanges, these must form a good face to face fit with the hull when the bracket has been set up in the installation position at the correct angle. This means of course, that the bearing centreline is in accurate alignment with the engine installation as previously described. If the alignment is not correct, a tapered hardwood pad bedded in mastic or a resin filler pad must be added between the hull and the bracket in order to correct the angle.

Inside the hull a thick plywood plate should be fitted, bedded on resin filler, to spread the load from the bracket bolts over a wider area. Initially only two of the holes will be drilled through the hull then the bracket fixed loosely so that the alignment can later be checked before finally drilling and bolting up the other holes.

From the drawing, measure the position where the shaft is to pass through the hull and mark accordingly. At this point, drill a hole large enough to allow a large round rasp or rotary rasp to be passed through. As the shaft is to pass through the hull at a shallow angle, the shape of the required hole on the surfaces will be elliptical.

To make the shaft outlet watertight either a shaft log or tube and gland can be used. Both the fittings have a greaser inlet and a packing gland on their inboard end. If fitting a shaft log, the hole through the hull only needs to be large enough to give good clearance for the shaft when all the alignment is complete. About $\frac{1}{8}$in to $\frac{1}{4}$in all round is adequate so begin by open-

ing the hole out with the rasp to give a rough alignment with the 'P' bracket. Remove the gland from the log and insert the shaft or piano wire through the 'P' bracket, up through the hull and shaft log and set up the alignment as previously described. You will now be able to see what is required for a bedding block under the shaft log. Make up a suitable bedding block from hardwood, fit and drill the block and the hull from the shaft log, refit the shaft to check the alignment and clearance. When all is correct, dismantle the assembly. Paint out the hole with resin, bed the block in resin putty, fit and finally bolt the shaft log into position.

Now, with the shaft, realign the 'P' bracket to the shaft log and when you are satisfied, bond the 'P' bracket and its plywood web securely into the hull. From this stage, make the engine bed template as described previously.

Where a tube fitting is to be employed, the hole through the hull must allow the tube to pass through. The inside of the hole should be chamfered to assist the resin impregnation. The

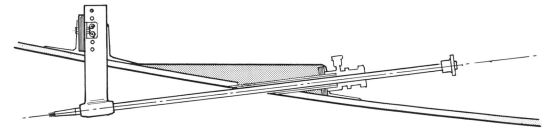

Fig 23   *Stern tube assembly for a light displacement boat with the outboard bearing supported in a 'P' bracket.*

inboard end of the tube has a gland fitting screwed on to it: this normally has a flange with two holes for bolting to the boat's structure as described under the heading 'Boats with propeller skegs'. Remove the gland, slip the tube over the shaft and set it in position so that it is concentric around the shaft. This can be achieved by using three small wooden wedges at each end between the shaft and tube. When the assembly has been set up correctly, cut a template and make a web to fit behind the gland fitting as previously described. From the outside, mark around the tube where it emerges from the hull. Dismantle the assembly, cut the excess tube off and bolt the gland to the web. Re-set the assembly as before. When the alignment is satisfactory, the web and the tube can be bonded strongly with three or four layers of fibreglass mat to the hull. Be sure to stipple the resin and fibreglass tightly around the tube, particularly underneath the forward end.

When the bonding has cured, it is a good plan to fill in the area aft of the web completely with fibreglass to form a solid, level block enclosing the tube. All your offcuts of fibreglass can be used for this. The easiest method of mixing up the filling material is to half fill a plastic bucket with resin and stir in the offcuts to make a good, stiff mix of resin and mat. You must have a high proportion of mat or the block will crack as it cures. When the fibreglass is fully soaked and mixed, add a handful of filler powder and stir it thoroughly. This is absolutely essential in such a quantity of resin and glass because as the

resin cures it will generate great heat and without the filler, it is very likely to catch fire. Lastly, add the catalyst and stir thoroughly. Mix the resin to cure at medium speed (a fast mix would generate more heat). Then tip the mix into place abaft the web and trowel it down with a piece of scrap timber to expel the air. Repeat the operation until the area is filled up level with the top of the web. As the block cures and begins to give off heat, keep a check on it to ensure that it does not catch fire. When the 'P' bracket and stern tube installation is complete, the engine bed template can be made as described under 'Boats with propeller skegs'.

Making the engine beds

There are many types and shapes of engine beds suitable for fibreglass boats, and it may be possible for you to buy a bed to suit your boat and engine from the hull manufacturer. However, if you wish to make your own, cut the two sides from timber about 2in thick to suit your template. These two shapes need only be roughly fashioned because they are only formers and when the bed is complete they will not be seen. The corners to the top edges and ends should be well rounded off to enable the fibreglass covering to follow their shape. Attach a wood block to the bottom of each former so that they can be held in a vice. With the former thus clamped, coat it liberally with resin and pre-cut pieces of 2oz chopped strand mat, and trim off any surplus fibreglass from the lower edges and tidy up generally. Remove the engine jig from the hull and position it on top of them. Check with the drawing or the engine itself to ensure that all parts of the engine, particularly the flywheel, will be clear of the bed when it is eventually mounted. From the bolt hole positions in the jig, spot through with a drill to mark the top of the bed blocks. Now you can remove the jig, drill right through the fibreglass

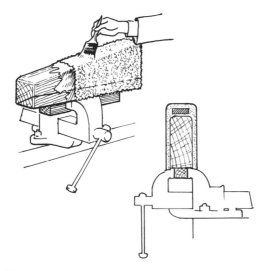

Fig 24 *Making fibreglass engine bed blocks using timber formers. Note the position of the steel insert.*

begin to build up a complete cover over the entire shape, including the ends, overlapping the joins in successive layers.

When you have built up about three layers all over, position a strip of mild steel (about $1\frac{1}{2}$in $\times \frac{3}{8}$in section to match the length of the former) on the top face in the wet resin, cover it with a good coat of resin and carry on as before, building up a further covering of at least another four layers over the entire assembly, encapsulating the steel strip. These steel 'inserts' are to form the anchorage for the engine fixing bolts. When the fibreglass is cured, build up the other half of the bed in the same way.

With the two halves of the bed complete,

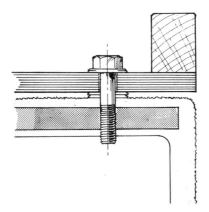

Fig 25 *Using spacing washers between the engine template and the bed blocks.*

and steel inserts with a drill at bolt core size, then tap and thread through to suit your engine fixing bolts. It is an advantage if these fixing bolts are somewhat slack in the engine feet as this will assist the alignment later. A $\frac{3}{8}$in bolt in a $\frac{1}{2}$in hole is about right.

Remove the two clamping blocks from the

bottoms of the bed blocks. Fit the jig into position on their top faces with two washers over each bolt hole to form spacers between the jig and the bed blocks. This will be used later as a packing space to achieve final alignment. If resilient mounts are to be used, these will be fitted between the jig and the beds at this stage in a similar way. The assembly can now be offered into the hull and set up with the rod or piano wire as before.

You might have to trim off the bottoms of the bed blocks to get the assembly right back into position or block it up slightly in order to align it accurately along the axis line. If you are using a steel rod for the alignment, make sure that the jig and bed assembly are not bearing their weight on it when set up, or the shaft will bend slightly causing misalignment problems. The position of the bed along the hull must be such that when the propeller shaft is finally installed, the propeller must be between $\frac{3}{4}$in to 1in clear of the outboard bearing when the gearbox is in neutral because some gearboxes allow the shaft to move slightly forward when going ahead and aft when going astern.

Check the jig for level across the hull, and when all is satisfactory, tack both sides of each block securely to the hull. When the tacking pieces have cured, remove the rod or wire, unbolt and remove the jig, and bond the bed finally into the hull. If you have room at the sides of the bed, cut and fit thick plywood webs to form lateral stiffening to the area: bond them into position as the bed is bonded. Build up sub-stantial fibreglass flanges about 4in up the sides of the bed and 4in onto the hull, tapering the successive layers back as you go.

At, or just forward of, the engine bed, cut and fit a plywood cross member about 4in deep and bond it to both the hull and the sides of the engine compartment. This will form a barrier to contain any spilt fuel or lubricating oil and prevent it from getting into the centre part of the boat.

Aligning the engine

When the stern tube bearing assembly and engine beds are complete and all the bondings cured, slide the propeller shaft into position then fit the inboard flange and the propeller.

Now the engine itself can be manoeuvred into position on the bed. If allowance has been made for resilient mounts, bolt them first to the engine feet. Now, if all the previous stages have been tackled successfully, you should find that when the engine feet are aligned over the bed, the holding bolts can be screwed in easily, but leave them loose. The centreline of the engine output flange should now be about $\frac{1}{16}$in below the centreline of the shaft flange.

You will then be able to raise the engine using a jemmy and inserting a series of thin metal shims beneath each of its feet until it is beginning to align with the shaft flange. Whilst this operation is in progress, keep an eye on it from above to check that it is in approximate alignment in both planes. Adjustment in this plane is made by sliding the engine slightly across the bed. Allowance has been made for this by having plenty of slack between the bolts and the holes. As the flanges begin to appear in alignment, use a 0·002in feeler gauge between them. This will clearly show what is left to be done to perfect the job. Finally, bolt the engine down tight, re-check the flanges and when all is well, smear them with grease and bolt them firmly together.

The alignment must be accurate whatever type of coupling is used or vibration, noise and wear will occur later. If a flexible coupling is to be fitted, the alignment must be made with a rigid coupling initially. It can then be removed and substituted with the flexible one. Some hulls tend to alter shape slightly when they are afloat so it is advisable to ensure that the alignment is still correct after launching. This is done by releasing the shaft coupling bolts and checking between the flanges again with the feeler gauge. If any change has taken place you will have to release the engine bolts and adjust the shims to suit.

16
Fuel Tanks and Supply Systems

Most hull manufacturers are able to either supply fuel tanks or recommend a supplier. The tank must be rigid and resistant to both damage and corrosion and is best made of stainless steel for these reasons. Ordinary steel tanks will quickly start to rust in the salt atmosphere, however well protected, and because they are usually mounted in an inaccessible position, they are not easy to keep well painted. Brass is sometimes used to hold petrol (gasolene) but is not suitable to contain diesel fuels because it reacts with them, causing a sludge to form.

Another possibility is to build your own fibreglass tank directly into the hull. This can be constructed in the same manner as a water tank, so we shall deal with them both later, bearing in mind the special features required for the fuel system. The size will probably be recommended on the drawing. This will be proportionate to the engine size and also the boat's displacement. It is a mistake to put too much capacity into a small boat because the fuel weight can easily upset the boat's trim. Sailing boats with small auxiliary engines usually carry about 5 to 10 gallons but power boats with large engines and no sails must carry enough to give adequate range commensurate with fuel consumption and the ability of the hull to carry the weight. As a guide:

1 cubic foot contains 6·25 gallons

1 cubic foot of petrol (gasolene) weighs approximately 46lbs

1 cubic foot of diesel fuel weighs approximately 53lbs

The essential features of a fuel tank are:-

1. Large (1½in to 2in diameter) fuel inlet tube over which a suitable reinforced plastic pipe can be clipped and led away to a compatible deckfitting which must be watertight. This plastic pipe must be completely fuel proof and secured at both ends so that fuel can be pumped or poured into the tank from the deck with no chance of spillage getting into the hull.

2. Sludge trap and drain cock. The sludge trap is a small projection at the lowest part of the tank which has a female thread to suit a draincock. This enables any sludge or water to settle below the outlet where it can be drained off.

3. Fuel outlet to the engine. This also has a female thread to suit a cock so that the fuel feed can be shut off for filter changing etc.

4. Vent. This is to allow air to enter as the fuel is used. A tube clipped to the vent is led away to a point well above the fuel level when the boat is at its maximum angle of roll or heel. This is to ensure that fuel is not ejected from the vent whilst the boat is at sea. The top end of the pipe should be hooked over like an umbrella handle to prevent dirt from entering.

5. Excess fuel return. If a diesel engine is fitted, an excess fuel return pipe is necessary. This is usually only about ¼in diameter and is linked to the tank from the injection pump via a plastic tube.

6. Baffle plates built across the inside of the tank to prevent fuel from surging from end to end whilst at sea.

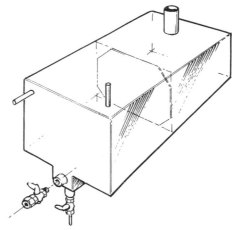

Fig 26   *A typical stainless steel fuel tank suitable for a diesel engine showing the internal baffle, fuel inlet, sludge trap and drain cock, fuel outlet and shut-off cock, back leak inlet and vent tube.*

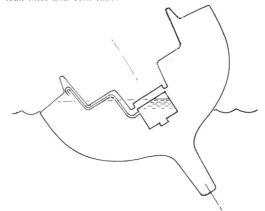

Fig 27   *It is essential to raise the level of the fuel vent outlet to prevent spillage when the boat heels or rolls.*

Siting the tank

The position of the fuel tank in the boat is governed by several factors: the type of boat, position of the engine, number of engines and the height of the carburettor or fuel pump. In most instances it will be an advantage, and sometimes a necessity, to fit the fuel tank before the engine is installed. For example, in a sailing boat with the engine and tank under the cockpit floor, it will be difficult to fit the tank after the engine, because of problems of access.

It must be sited so that the outlet is at least at the same height, preferably 2in or 3in above the level of the carburettor or injection pump to give sufficient gravity feed. If this is not possible, an electric pump similar to the type used in cars must be fitted in the fuel feed pipe close to the tank outlet.

Pipework to the engine

This should be made in either copper or steel bundy tube for best strength and resilience to knocks. All the pipe fitting joint faces should be coated with a fuel proof jointing compound before assembly and the pipe clipped securely to the adjacent structure at intervals of about 9in. A suitable filter should be fitted in the system in a reasonably accessible position. For a diesel engine this should be of the replaceable paper element type giving a high degree of filtration. The filter must be bolted to the adjacent structure and not left supported only on the pipework.

The metal pipework should be joined to the carburettor or injection pump by a 6in to 12in length of braided wire or steel armoured fuel proof tube, clipped securely at both ends. This is to ensure that engine vibration will not fracture the fuel pipe, particularly for engines installed on resilient mounts. Never forget that fuel leakage into the bilges can lead to explosion and fire. These are extremely serious hazards on a boat, so great care must be taken in fitting the fuel system.

17

Exhausts

As with the fuel tank, the exhaust system should also be fitted before too much joinery is fixed into the aft part of the boat to avoid access problems. The outlet fitting should be fitted through the stern, just above the waterline, rather than through the side of the hull. This will prevent the exhaust from making unsightly stains down the side of the hull. There are two types of system, wet or dry.

Wet systems

Most small marine engines have wet systems, in which the cooling water discharges into the exhaust pipe. After passing through the cylinder head, the cooling water should be piped up well above the boat's waterline and then back down into the exhaust pipe just below the manifold or exhaust chamber level. At the highest point of the pipe, a vacuum relief valve should be fitted to ensure that the cylinders cannot flood after the engine has been stopped. This system has a threefold advantage in that it cools the exhaust gas, reduces the noise and can be made up from rubber pipe. Since the heavy duty reinforced rubber pipes are easy to fit, they can be made to follow the chosen route in one continuous length. They have a further noise dampening effect so that, with the smaller engines, a silencer may not be necessary.

At the outlet end, a gate valve or seacock should precede the skin fitting so that the outlet can be closed off in an emergency. The pipe

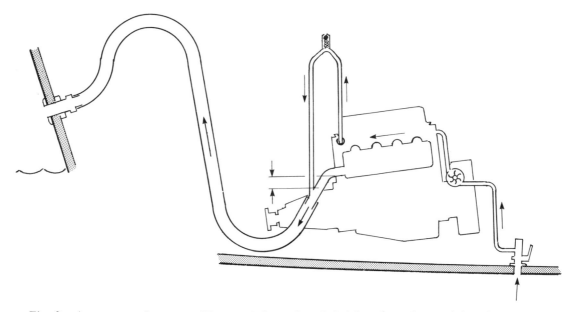

Fig 28 *A sea water cooling system. The water is drawn through the inlet valve and pumped through the waterways in the cylinder head. It is then piped into the exhaust pipe via a vacuum relief valve situated above the waterline.*

must be well secured to the exhaust manifold and the seacock, using a heat resistant jointing compound and hose clips. Run the pipe from the engine along the bottom of the hull and, as it approaches the stern, arrange it in a vertical 'swan-neck' which rises well above the waterline before descending again to the seacock. This is to prevent sea-water from entering the pipe from outside and thus flooding the engine.

The pipe should be clipped or bracketed to the adjoining structure at intervals of about 4ft to prevent movement and chafe. This is particu-

larly important in the vicinity of the exposed part of the propeller shaft. If a silencer is to be fitted, it must be supported at both ends. Rubber silencers are available and are preferable because they do not need lagging. If a metal silencer is used it must be supported clear of any combustible material and lagged.

Dry systems

These require metal exhaust pipes in order to

cope with the heat (the cooling water is discharged overboard through its own separate pipe). These metal systems are not usually fitted by amateur builders because they require special skills and equipment to make and fit. They must be fitted and bracketed in such a way that exhaust heat cannot be transmitted to the hull or woodwork. This is achieved with asbestos mounting blocks, and the entire system must be lagged with asbestos string. This can be overlaid with asbestos tape or stitched in asbestos cloth to improve the appearance and add a little more resistance to damage. When exhaust pipes of this type pass through lockers they should be protected by a guard to prevent combustible items such as ropes or sails being laid on them.

18
Electrics

The electrical installation for most small craft can be conveniently sub-divided into two main sections. These are the primary circuit, normally supplied in kit form with the engine, and the secondary or service circuit which supplies all the instruments, interior lights and navigation lights.

A careful study of the circuit diagram shown in the engine handbook should enable you to connect up the equipment correctly. Initially, make sure that you identify each piece of equipment as being the same as is shown in the handbook because engine manufacturers have a peculiar habit of changing specifications and not handbooks. If this is so, you may have to get some advice from the manufacturer, the engine agent or perhaps some direct assistance from your garage electrician.

Generally, the terminals on each of the component parts will be marked with a letter or symbol which is also indicated on the diagram. The cable identification colours may be marked, so connecting up is somewhat simpler than it may at first appear. A typical circuit is shown in fig 29.

The primary circuit

This is the circuit needed by the engine itself, which is simply an engine driven generating system connected to a lead/acid battery. The generator can be either a plain dynamo, an alternator or a dynamo-starter combined. Most

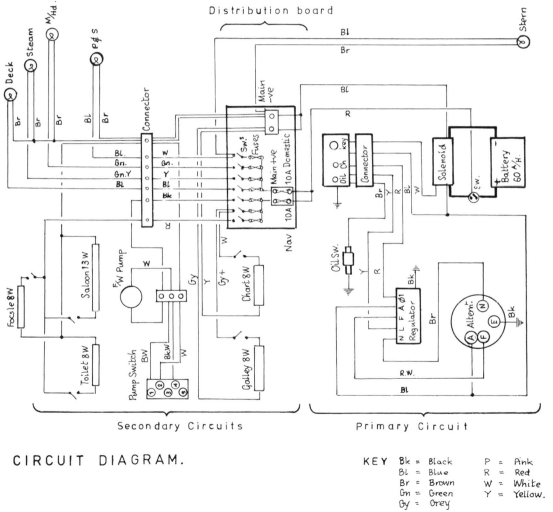

CIRCUIT DIAGRAM.

KEY	Bk = Black	P = Pink
	Bl = Blue	R = Red
	Br = Brown	W = White
	Gn = Green	Y = Yellow.
	Gy = Grey	

Fig 29 *A typical circuit diagram showing the primary generating circuit, the battery and the secondary circuit.*

generating machines are polarity sensitive so correct connection of the leads to the regulator and the battery is essential to prevent permanent damage. Alternators are particularly sensitive in this respect and the leads must never be disconnected whilst the engine is running or when any circuit is switched on.

The primary wiring sets are usually supplied with the cables made up into a 'harness', ready to connect up. The ends are fitted with forks or eyes to suit the appropriate terminals. The heavy cables supplied are to connect the battery to the starter. These take very heavy electrical load so good connections here are essential. Each cable end should be smeared with vaseline before final fitting to keep corrosion at bay and finally, when the primary circuit is complete, clip all the cables neatly to the adjoining structure.

Batteries

The primary function of the battery is to provide power to start the engine and, if it is a petrol (gasolene) engine, to supply the ignition system. The battery capacity required for these purposes will be recommended in the engine handbook. Additional capacity is required if all the other lighting services are to be adequately supplied. The capacity is expressed in Ampere/Hours (A/H) and, in order to evaluate the additional capacity required, you must decide how much power will be consumed on average between occasions when the engine is used.

The power consumed by each item of equipment is specified in Watts. These must be converted into Amperes by using the following formula:

$$\frac{\text{Watts}}{\text{Volts}} = \text{Amperes}$$

Most systems are 12 Volts and therefore a 12 Volt lamp of 6 Watts will consume:

$$\frac{6\ \text{Watts}}{12\ \text{Volts}} = 0\cdot5\ \text{Amps}$$

Make a table showing the items selected and their consumption to calculate the extra capacity requirement as follows:

Item	Consumption (amps)	Period (hrs)	Total (amps)
Riding light	1·0	10	10
Saloon lamp	1·0	3	3
Galley lamp	0·5	2	1
Focsle lamp	0·5	1	0·5
Under way			
Port and starboard lights	2·0	3	6
Stern light	1·0	3	3

Therefore additional capacity = 23·5 Amps

So if, for example, the battery capacity recommended for starting purposes is 60 A/H, you will need a battery of about 85 A/H to start the engine after a night at anchor using power at this rate, particularly in cold weather.

The battery should be sited as close to the

starter as possible to keep the leads short commensurate with accessibility. It must be kept
dry and well ventilated, to allow hydrogen to
escape whilst it is being charged by the generator.

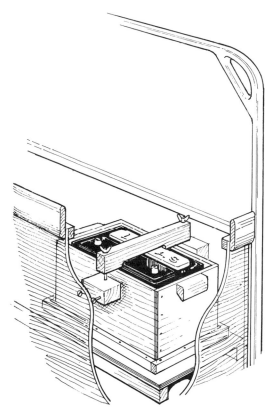

Fig 30   *The battery clamped in an acid proof box provided with strong handles to facilitate easy removal.*

Electrolyte from the battery must not be
allowed to spill anywhere in the boat, so to avoid
this, mount it in a stout plywood box which
has been painted inside and out with two generous coats of polyester resin. The whole assembly
must be made and positioned so that it cannot
move when the boat is at sea and must also be
relatively easily accessible. It is a good plan to
make strong handles on the box so that it can be
lifted out complete with the battery if necessary.

For good battery performance always:

1 Keep the battery well charged.
2 Keep it clean
3 Smear the terminals with vaseline.
4 Maintain the electrolyte level with distilled
  water.

The secondary circuits

These are best sub-divided again into separate
supplies for each of the main facilities such as
navigation lights, domestic lights and instruments (if fitted).

They can all come from one distribution board
which will be supplied from the positive terminal
via a master isolating switch. A main fuse should
be provided for each facility (Nav. lights,
Interior, etc). Then from these fuses, each individual circuit will be supplied via its own fuse
and switch. This will ensure that if a fault
occurs on any one of the circuits, the others
will remain functional; a valuable feature at

night. The negative return cables from each circuit can be connected to a common terminal block and then back to the battery through a single cable. The main positive feed and negative return cables must be capable of carrying the entire electrical load when all the circuits are working.

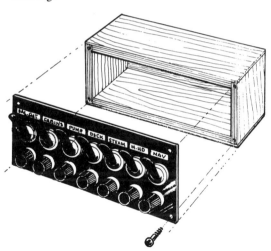

Fig 31 *A distribution box containing pop-in fuses and car-type switches. The supply from the battery is wired in through the back to the 'Navigation' and 'Domestic' main fuses. These feed the individual circuits via the circuit fuses and switches.*

You can purchase the distribution box complete with all the switches and fuses, but it is quite simple to make your own, using plywood for the sides and ends, and a piece of laminated plastic sheet for the fascia. Matt black gives a professional appearance, particularly with a neat label to identify each switch.

Car-type single pole switches and 'pop-in' line fuses mounted through the fascia can be connected from the main positive fuses to each circuit. These switches and fuses are readily available in car accessory and radio shops. The fuse ratings should be about double the full load current for each circuit.

Before starting the secondary wiring, draw a diagram of the proposed circuits. This will help you to form a clear picture of your objectives and save time on the job. Work to the diagram using cables with a variety of colour coded plastic insulation covers and mark the diagram with the codes as you go. In this way, each circuit can be identified if a fault develops later on. When the work is complete, keep the diagram for future reference; perhaps glue it under the lid of your battery box, or inside a cupboard.

Cable selection

In low voltage circuits, care must be taken to avoid causing too much voltage drop by using cables of small cross sectional area for long runs. The voltage drop should not exceed 4% overall; that is only 0·5 volts on a 12 volt system. You will in any case, lose about 0·25 volts between the battery and the distribution box via the fuses and switches. Relatively heavy cables must therefore be used to supply equipment which is sited far from the battery, otherwise efficiency will be impaired. This will be aggravated if the battery is in a low state of charge, to the extent that some equipment, such as fluorescent lamps, may not work at all. The items which most commonly suffer from this malaise are mast lights in sailing boats. On a 30ft craft, the total circuit length from the distribution panel to the masthead lamp and back can be around 100ft. The table below shows the maximum circuit lengths of cable of given size that can be used for carrying various amperages without suffering unacceptable voltage drop. If for example, you fit a masthead tricolour navigation light, this could have a 25 watt bulb taking 2·1 amps. From the table below it can be seen that this will require a 97/·3 cable.

CIRCUIT LENGTH IN FEET FOR 0·25 VOLT DROP MAX

Cable Size	Current *(amps)*			
Conductors, Size mm	*1*	*3*	*5*	*10*
14/·25	30	10	6	—
14/·3	45	15	9	—
21/·3	65	20	13	7
28/·3	85	30	17	9
35/·3	110	35	21	11
44/·3	135	45	27	13
65/·3	200	70	40	20
84/·3	260	85	52	26
97/·3	300	100	60	30

However, as most of the domestic circuits are relatively short and carry less than 1 amp, you may find it convenient to use car trailer cable from the distribution box to a junction box placed fairly centrally within the accommodation. In this way, a number of colour coded cables can be run behind the joinery in one neat outer sheath.

Lamps, pumps and instruments

The connection of lamps with ordinary filament bulbs is fairly foolproof, but just about all the other equipment needs more care. Each item normally has its own switch which will be connected to the positive supply and also its own wiring details in the form of a pamphlet when purchased or a wiring diagram inside the lid. Many items, such as fluorescent lamps, are polarity sensitive, so again you must make sure that the positive and negative cables are correctly connected or the equipment will be ruined.

The ferrule of each bulb should be smeared with vaseline before fitting as with all the other connections. Without this, they can fail through corrosion and can be surprisingly difficult to remove.

19
Hull Fittings

Great care must be taken to ensure that the materials used for all underwater fittings and their fastenings are similar in order to prevent the occurrence of electrolysis. See chapter 11, fastenings.

Pipe fittings

Fig 32   Hull pipe fittings a) plain skin fitting for use above the waterline. b) skin fitting and gate valve for general applications below the waterline. c) cone valve designed for fitting direct on to the hull, used mainly for WC soil pipes. d) cooling water inlet valve with rodding cap.

These must be made entirely in brass or bronze with no internal iron or steel parts. Ideally they should be fastened to the hull with machine screws of naval brass or silicon bronze, but it is now common practice to use stainless steel

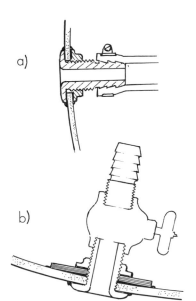

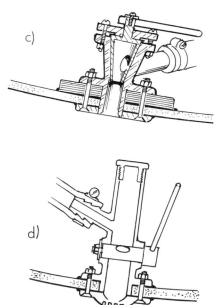

machine screws, which are an acceptable alternative.

A variety of pipe fittings are required for the inlets and outlets for the different facilities within the hull. Each one must be either a valve, or fitted directly with a valve so that the opening can be closed off when the boat is left unattended. This is important because the pipework is generally of reinforced plastic, and although this is a reliable material, any leakage could sink the boat.

The fittings are all specified by their bore size. The following table shows a typical selection of the types and applications.

The position of each fitting is determined by the equipment to which it is connected and also the access for controlling the valves. Recommended positions are usually indicated on the instructions pamphlets supplied with toilets etc, and these will be influenced by the adjacent joinery. Having selected suitable positions, it is advisable to drill a small pilot hole through the hull from the inside.

Opening the holes up to the required sizes is best done with a hole saw or tank cutter driven by an electric drill. These require considerable torque because of the large diameter of the bit and the tendency of fibreglass to clog, so you will need one of the more powerful drills, or the armature will burn out. Work from the outside to avoid damaging the gel-coat.

The fitting flanges must be made to fit snugly on to the face of the hull to ensure a reliable watertight joint. This may mean that the area will need flattening with a disc cutter, and if this has the effect of significantly thinning the hull, you will have to build it up on the inside with fibreglass or a wooden pad to reinforce the area. If the fitting has bolt flanges, use it as a jig to mark the bolt positions. Then remove it, drill the bolt holes through the hull and countersink the outside if necessary.

Function	Typical Size	Fitting Type	Remarks
Galley sink outlet	$\frac{1}{2}$in	Screwed skinfitting with collar nut and hose connector	Above W.L. (No valve)
Gas bottle locker overflow	$\frac{1}{2}$in		
Bilge pump outlet	$1\frac{1}{4}$in		
Cockpit drains	$1\frac{1}{2}$in	Screwed skinfitting with collar nut	Fitted with gatevalve
Exhaust pipe outlet	$1\frac{3}{4}$in		
Toilet flushing inlet	$\frac{3}{4}$in		
Toilet soil outlet	$1\frac{3}{4}$in	Cone cock	Fitted direct
Engine cooling inlet	$\frac{1}{2}$in	Valve with rodding tube	Fitted direct

When the holes have been prepared, paint out the bores and faces with resin to seal the cut edge of the fibreglass and prevent water from entering the material by means of capillary action. Every fitting must be bedded and tightened down in marine mastic to form a permanent watertight joint with the hull.

Good quality reinforced plastic pipes are required for the plumbing systems of boats. These are made so that they are resistant to kinking when they are bent and therefore have stiff, thick walls. This often makes them difficult to get on to the fittings. If this is so, smear the fitting end with soap and soak the end of the pipe in boiling water for about ten minutes to soften it. Then, using rubber gloves, quickly push the pipe well on to the fitting and secure it with a hose clip.

Echo sounder transducers

These days most boats are fitted with an echo sounder. The installation instructions supplied with the instrument will recommend the most reliable position for mounting the transducer, but not much detail of how best to make a good, sound job in a fibreglass hull. For obvious reasons, the best position is well forward, on the centreline of the boat. It must be mounted in a vertical position, clear of the most turbulent water flow areas, and so not too near the bow. In most sailing craft this means just forward of the keel.

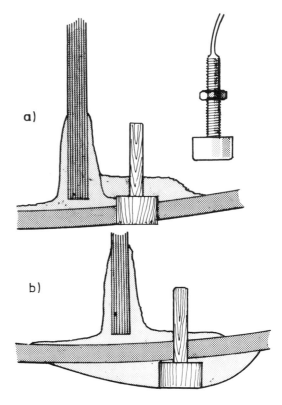

Fig 33 *Making a housing for the echo sounder transducer using a wooden replica. a) flush mounting. b) blister mounting.*

The head of the transducer must be protected from floating debris, so it must be either sunk into the hull until its face is flush or else be mounted in a 'blister'. As with all skin fittings, select the mounting position from the inside with reference to the bulkheads etc, and drill a small pilot hole to ensure that all is well, and to determine the hull thickness in the area.

Now a through hole with a counterbore has to be created in the hull, into which the transducer head and shank will fit. As the hull is not likely to be more than about $\frac{3}{4}$in thick in the area, it is not possible to fit the transducer without modification to the hull. The best method is to make a wooden replica of the transducer and set it in the required position to mould around its shape in fibreglass. Making the replica using a lathe is simple but otherwise you will have to carefully fashion it by hand. It should be about $\frac{1}{16}$in larger in diameter than the transducer itself. When it is finished, coat it generously with car or furniture polish to prevent resin adhesion.

Bore right through the hull to suit the replica head and paint the sides of the hole with resin. Set the replica in place using props to support it from the outside and then build up a thick pad of fibreglass on the inside, making sure that it is stippled tightly on to the head and around the shank. After it has cured, knock the replica out and grind the top of the pad off flat and square to the bore, to form a seating face for the transducer nut.

If you prefer to make a blister mounting, the method will be similar, except that the hull will be bored to suit the replica shank and you will need to cut back the hull gel-coat in the area to provide a suitable surface upon which to build. The blister can then be made around the replica on the outside with offcuts of fibreglass as required and then trimmed to a good streamlined shape with a disc when it is fully cured.

On no account use the transducer itself to make this moulding, because you will never be able to remove it subsequently. Use plenty of mastic to fit the transducer and do not over-tighten the nut.

20

Deck Fittings

The deck fittings should, as far as possible, be fitted before the joinery and headlinings, so that washers and nuts can be fitted on the inside. This is particularly necessary on any fittings which are to carry load and also for pulpits, stanchions, etc, which may have to carry a sudden load.

Pulpits, stanchions, toe rails, etc

These are all fittings which must be capable of withstanding moderate shock load without breaking away from the deck. The bases are usually drilled to suit $\frac{1}{4}$in diameter machine screws.

From your deckplan drawing, mark out their positions and using each one as a drill guide, spot through their fixing holes with a drill. Remove the fitting and drill through the deck at screw core size, then cut the required threads through with a tap. To save time, professional boatbuilders often force stainless steel machine screws through unthreaded core holes in fibreglass using a carpenter's brace and screwdriver bit. In this way, the machine screw cuts its own thread, but this method should not be used with screws under $\frac{1}{4}$in diameter or they will break.

It is preferable to drill and thread the holes for all machine screw fixings through fibreglass. This in itself gives a surprisingly strong fastening, but when backed up by a washer and a nut on the inside makes a really sound, watertight job.

Check with the fitting that the holes are in the right place and then coat its bottom face and the machine screws with mastic. Screw it down tightly then fit the nuts and washers on the inside. A neat professional touch is given if you align all the screwdriver slots with the fore and aft line of the boat. As you tighten up the nuts on the inside, you will need an assistant on deck with a screwdriver to prevent the screws from rotating.

Chainplates

These are the fittings to which the shrouds are attached on a sailing craft. The chainplates and their attachments to the hull must be capable of carrying the very high strain imposed by the rig when under sail. It should be possible to lift the craft up by the chainplates on both sides.

On smaller craft, these are sometimes in the form of a 'U' bolt with a welded deckplate. The 'U' bolt is fitted through the deck and also through a thick plywood pad, bedded on to the underside of the deck to spread the load.

Larger boats, particularly racing designs, need much more strength in this area and therefore the chainplate load must be transferred totally from the deck to the hull. This can be achieved in a variety of ways, but the most common is to bond a stout web of fibreglass or thick ply into the corner formed by the deck and the hull adjacent to each chainplate. The chainplates have tangs which pass through the deck, or

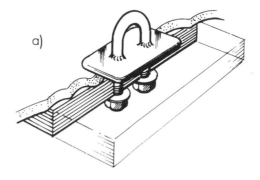

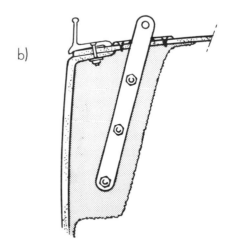

Fig 34 *Chainplates. a) 'U' bolt with deckplate and reinforcing pad under the deck. b) with bonded web to transfer the strain to the hull.*

inner tangs which bolt to the chainplate through the deck. These are bolted to the webs. Backstay fittings are fitted in a similar manner.

Bow fittings

On motor boats and small sailing craft, these are often just bolted through the deck, as with chainplates. Larger sailing craft must have bow fittings which transfer the load to the hull itself by way of a stem tang or an internal link to a stem plate.

Cleats, sheet tracks and winches

These are all high load fittings which must have bolts through the deck fitted with washers and nuts on the inside. Many fibreglass deck mouldings are constructed of two skins with a soft middle layer made of end grain balsa wood blocks. This double skin covers only the wide, flat areas to help support a person's weight anywhere on deck. If any high load fitting is to be mounted on these areas, the inner skin and core must be cut away with a 1in drill bit or hole saw so that each washer and nut will seat firmly under the outer skin. This is essential to prevent the fastenings or fitting load crushing the soft core. Each bolt or machine screw thread must be coated with mastic before final fitting to ensure that they will not leak when load is applied to the fitting.

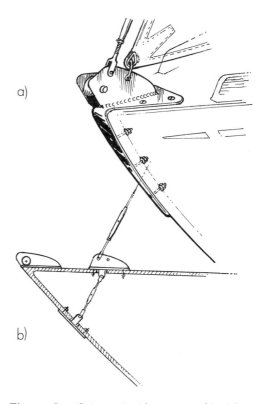

Fig 35 *Bow fittings. a) with stem tang. b) with stem plate and internal screw tensioner.*

Windows

For fibreglass craft there are three basic types:-

1 Transparent plastic sheet, mounted direct.
2 Transparent plastic or laminated glass in rubber surround.
3 Toughened glass in aluminium frame.

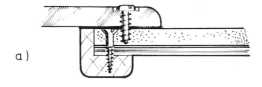

a)

b)

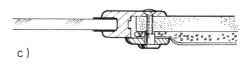

c)

Fig 36 *Window details. a) plastic sheet window with ply lining bonded to the inside of the deck moulding with a timber surround. b) rubber mounted. c) aluminium framed with soft lining under internal frame.*

The choice is influenced by personal preference, availability and cost. The hull moulder will be able to supply or recommend windows to suit your boat. Whichever type you choose, you must decide before beginning to fit them, what method of finishing is to be employed around the inside, as this may affect the sequence of operations. This again depends on whether the boat already has a fibreglass headlining or not. We shall deal with making headlinings and hull panellings later, but in the meantime, the sketches show the problem and some possible solutions.

When you have obtained the windows, mark out their positions on the outside of the superstructure with a wax crayon. Initially, it is best to place the windows one by one on the superstructure in the desired positions, and mark

Fig 37 *Ensure that the windows are all in alignment before cutting the deck moulding.*

around the outside edges. You can then stand back to inspect and check that the positions and alignment are satisfactory, before finally marking the sizes of the openings to be cut. These are determined by the type of windows to be fitted and are obviously smaller than the flange sizes.

Drill through the superstructure, about $\frac{3}{8}$in

diameter, on the waste side of the lines, to insert your jigsaw blade. You will need several fine toothed blades to cut around all the openings because fibreglass is very abrasive, causing the blades to wear out very quickly.

A lot of dust is made on this job so it is as well to complete it before getting started on the joinery inside. If the engine is already fitted, cover it up before you start the sawing. When the openings have been cut, you can tape pieces of polythene sheet over them to keep rain out, if there is likely to be any delay in fitting the windows.

Plastic sheet windows

These are the most simple type. You can make these at home from the raw material using simple tools and so they are relatively cheap. They are made from acrylic plastic sheet, usually $\frac{3}{8}$in thick and fitted on a mastic bedding directly to the superstructure. The material can be either clear or, for extra effect, tinted, and is supplied with protective paper coverings on each face. The windows should be marked out on these covers whilst they are in place. Then they can be cut out with the jigsaw with minimum risk of being scratched. They are attached to the superstructure by stainless steel round head self tapping or machine screws, spaced at about 3in centres. These can also be marked on the paper faces $\frac{1}{2}$in from the edge so that the windows can overlap the openings by 1in all round. Do not

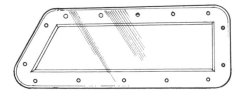

Fig 38 *Plastic sheet window with radius corners mounted over an aperture with angular corners to simplify the internal frame.*

use countersunk screws because the conical heads may tend to split the plastic.

The corners should have a radius of only about 1in in order to simplify the internal trim and the edges rounded on the outside face. Don't forget that if the windows are to have an asymmetric shape, they must also be port and starboard handed. The plastic can be cut to shape with a fine toothed handsaw or jigsaw, but must be well supported whilst being worked to avoid cracking. The edges are best rounded with a router or a sharp plane, and then refined stage by stage, using first a file and then progressively finer abrasive papers. Final polishing with metal polish or car body cutting compound will remove all the tool and sanding marks and make the edges completely transparent to match the faces.

Windows of this type are commonly fitted to boats without plastic headlinings. In this case it is normal to cover the inside of the superstructure with either thin ply or foam backed vinyl and fit a moulded hardwood surround to finish off the window inside. In order to simplify the surround, it is advisable that the openings have angular rather than radiused corners (see fig 38).

Rubber mounted windows

These are fitted to small, simple craft where no linings are required. The rubber strip surround has a groove on one edge to suit the thickness of the glass and a groove on the other edge to suit the plastic superstructure. They are relatively cheap but not particularly smart.

They have radiused corners and the openings into which they fit must be cut fairly accurately to accommodate the glass and the rubber strip. The rubber is first fitted tightly around the glass and cut to length to form an accurate butt joint. Sealing compound is necessary between the glass and the rubber and also between the rubber and the superstructure to prevent leakage.

The assembly is then fitted by bending the outer lip back whilst it is eased into place. Finally an insert is fitted into the groove on the outside face of the rubber to secure it.

Aluminium framed windows

Undoubtedly the best for quality, appearance and a good, reliable job from the practical viewpoint. They are made in toughened glass or clear plastic, set in an extruded aluminium frame with a broad flange around the outside, through which they are fastened to the superstructure. They are suitable for craft with or without internal linings.

The openings through the superstructure (and internal fibreglass lining if fitted) are cut to suit the spigot size of the frame. It is neither practicable nor necessary to achieve an accurate fit here because the frame must, in any case, be bedded in mastic and the internal trim will cover the joint. The fastenings will be stainless steel self tapping or machine screws.

Some windows of this type are supplied with aluminium trims which fit inside and form an anchorage for the fixing screws. These trims also make a neat covering to the edge of the internal lining. This means that the internal lining must be fitted before the trims.

If the boat already has an internal plastic lining, there is usually a gap of between $\frac{1}{2}$in to 1in between this and the inside of the superstructure moulding. In order to make a neat job of fitting the windows it is necessary to secure the two mouldings here. This can be done by trowelling resin putty in the gap and clamping them together around the opening. A plywood surround that overlaps the outer edge of the window frame will provide a suitable trim to cover the join. This can be attached to the lining with small self tapping screws.

Bilge pumps

These must be installed so that they can be

reached and operated by the helmsman. In sailing craft they are usually situated on the side
of the cockpit well or the coaming. The best
type is designed to fit behind the panel to
which it is mounted. The detachable operating
lever protrudes through the panel via a flexible,
watertight gaiter. This means that the pump
itself is mounted out of sight inside a locker and
will therefore not encumber the cockpit. Whatever pump is fitted, you must leave clear access
to it so that the cover can be removed quickly
in the event of it becoming choked.

21

Deck Joinery

On most fibreglass craft, this is limited to grab-rails, hatches and minor trim. This is to minimise the cost of such work on professionally finished boats. Many designs have moulded projections to form winch, grabrail and cleat bases, and so on, leaving only simple woodwork to finish off.

Hardwood must be used for all exposed woodwork, and it is often finished in bright varnish. If you wish to avoid the chore of annual revarnishing you must use either teak or afrormosia, as these are about the only popular timbers that are able to withstand the marine environment without the protection of paint or varnish. They can be left to weather naturally, in which case they turn silver grey in colour or they can be treated with teak oil occasionally, which tends to make them darken.

Main hatches

These are usually in the form of a hatch or lid which slides on runners. The vertical part of the hatchway is enclosed by double doors or sliding washboards. Many craft are supplied with fibreglass hatches which are designed to slide on rails moulded integrally with the superstructure. The detail drawings will show what arrangements are intended for these.

Assuming that the hatches are not supplied, we will describe what has to be achieved with the construction in general terms. Mouldings are often supplied with no openings for the

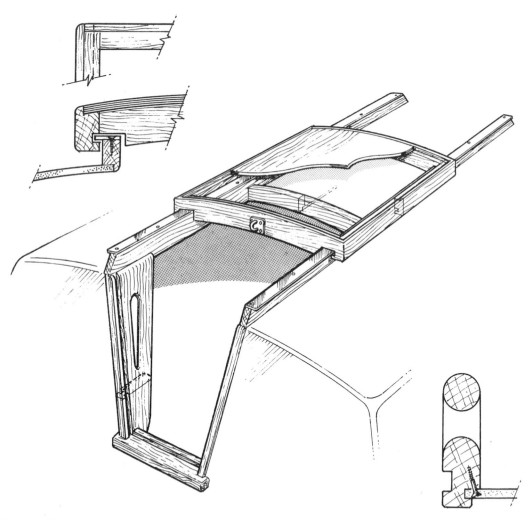

Fig 39   *Wooden hatch construction. The sides of the entrance are integral with the grab handles, and the stopwater at the forward end of the opening also forms a stop for the hatch at each end of its travel.*

hatchway so they must be marked out in accordance with the design and cut out, allowing for the thickness of the framework. The runners are mounted on hardwood rails which form the sides of the hatchway opening. The rails are attached by woodscrews from the inside of the coachroof or, if a headlining is fitted, by machine screws through the rail into the roof.

The runners, which guide and retain the hatch, project into grooves on the inside of its frame. They are made of brass or plastic strip and they are attached to the rails with countersunk woodscrews. The grooves on the inside edges of the hatch frame must be a generous clearance fit on the runners or the hatch will jam when wet. At the forward end of the hatchway, a water bar is required between the two rails. This is to prevent water from driving under the hatch, and also to form the end stop.

The hatch itself must be built accurately to suit this assembly. It is basically a frame with cambered cross members. If the corners are joined using half lap joints and the top edges are rebated to house a cambered ply top about $\frac{3}{8}$in thick, virtually all end grain will be concealed (see fig 39). This makes a strong, thoroughly professional looking job which will retain its varnish well. For the real luxury job, the ply top can be sheathed with close fitting hardwood slats. These are much more durable than ply which, when used externally, tends to shed its varnish rather quickly. The inside of the top can be lined with laminated plastic to give a good, permanent finish.

The vertical opening framework consists of two side pieces and a rebated sill which are all grooved at the back to fit snugly over the edge of the fibreglass. These are arranged so that the side pieces, which are attached with woodscrews through the fibreglass, lock the sill in position (see fig 39). They can also incorporate grab handles on the inside to assist people to get in and out of the hatchway.

For washboards, it is normal to make the opening with tapered sides and grooved side pieces to enable the boards to be fitted or removed easily. For double doors, the sides need only a rebated section to form a jamb or stop, similar to the sill.

Washboards are made from plywood, about $\frac{5}{8}$in or $\frac{3}{4}$in thick, edged with matching hardwood. They also need a good clearance fit in the frame-grooves. The top and bottom edges need a bevel to prevent water from running between them into the cabin. A simple hasp and staple fitting with a padlock will secure the hatch to the top washboard. The hasp must be fitted to the washboard and not the hatch. If it is fitted to the hatch, somebody may catch their head on it.

Double doors can also be made in $\frac{5}{8}$in ply with an edging strip. The two meeting edges should be rebated to form an overlap when the doors are closed so the strips should be wider here to incorporate the rebate. The hinges used for these doors are usually the lift-off type so that the doors can be removed and stowed away whilst cruising in good weather.

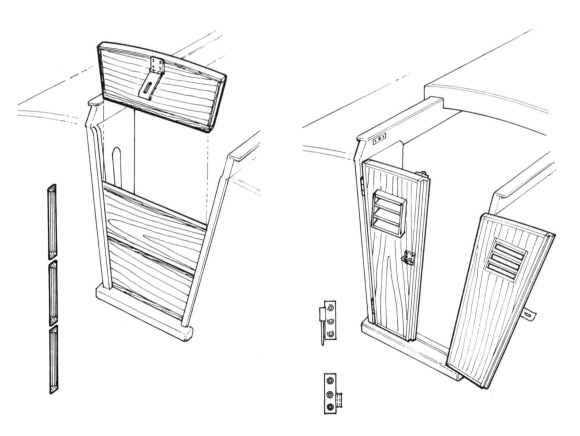

Fig 40 *Washboards which fit into grooves at the sides of the hatchway. The top and bottom edges of the boards are chamfered to prevent water from running into the cabin.*

Fig 41 *Double doors with an overlap rebate. They are usually hung on lift-off hinges which permit easy removal.*

To secure a hatchway with double doors it is necessary to secure the hatch first with a pair of barrel bolts fitted inside which lock it to the rails, then secure one door with a barrel bolt at the top and the bottom. The doors are then padlocked with a hasp and staple.

Forehatches

Most boats have a square, flat area on the superstructure for the fitting of the forehatch. It will often be found that the size of this corresponds with a particular manufacturer's standard aluminium framed forehatch. These hatches are simple to fit because they need only a hole of the required size and shape, cut through the superstructure. The frame is then bedded in mastic and attached with machine screws in the normal way. There may also be a rim supplied which can be fitted around the inside of the frame to cover the edge of the fibreglass and the lining.

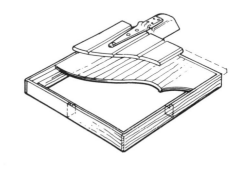

Fig 43 *Construction details for a wooden forehatch fitted to a deck moulding with a raised coaming. The gasket seats on the upper part of the coaming.*

Many craft have their hatchway moulded into the superstructure. These are often designed for a wooden forehatch to be fitted. The construction must be able to withstand the hatch being slammed and, particularly in sailing craft, a person's weight, because it is near the mast–a centre of activity. The frame is made to suit the section of the moulded surround (see fig 43) and the top, from plywood at least $\frac{1}{2}$in thick. The top can with advantage be fitted into a rebate in the frame and sheathed with hardwood slats as recommended for main hatches.

To make the hatchway watertight, a soft rubber gasket must be fitted in a rebate around the inside of the frame so that when the hatch

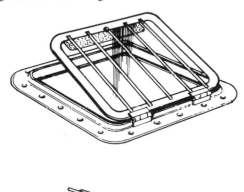

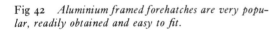

Fig 42 *Aluminium framed forehatches are very popular, readily obtained and easy to fit.*

is closed and fastened, the gasket will seat tightly on the inner edge of the surround. The outside edge of the frame must therefore not be in contact with the deck moulding.

The positioning of the hinges is crucial in achieving a watertight seal. These hinges are often fitted on wood spacing blocks, which should be arranged so that the gasket along the hinge edge comes into contact with the plastic surround. Two toggle fasteners should be fitted to the opposite inside edge of the hatch to pull it down tight from the inside. As with the main hatch, a laminated plastic lining inside the lid will add the final touch.

Grabrails

These are an important safety feature on any craft. They must be strong, easy to grip and firmly fixed. They must be made of hardwood that is completely free from knots, splits and shakes. They are usually varnished.

Some coachrooves have integrally moulded raised blocks to form a base for straight grabrails. These are simply lengths of rectangular section hardwood with generous radii along all the edges. They require mastic bedding and fastening with stainless steel machine screws set in counterbores which are then pelleted. A pellet is similar to a short length of dowel except that the grain runs across the diameter and not along the axis. They are cut in matching timber from an offcut of the work in progress using a special

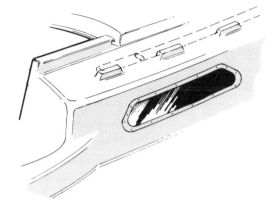

Fig 44 *A deck moulding incorporating raised blocks to simplify the grabrails.*

cutter. They are less obtrusive than dowels because they blend with the timber (see tool appendix).

If making complete grabrails, you will need to prepare hardwood strips of about 1in × 2in section to the required lengths. To look right, all the cut-outs must be identical, so it is worth making a marking out template.

The top part of the rail should be rounded in section, about 1in diameter minimum and the length of the cut-out pieces between 6in to 8in long with 3in to 4in legs in between.

Using a centrebit of 1in diameter in an electric drill, bore the timber at each end of the cut-out. Keep the bores clear from the edge of the timber to avoid feather edging, and bore into the timber until the bit centre breaks through. Then, to avoid splitting, bore in from the opposite side to finish the holes. The pieces can then be cut out and the ends profiled using a jigsaw.

The quickest method of rounding the cut-outs, the top edges and the ends is with a router. If you do not have one of these, the job will have to be done using a round backed rasp, spokeshave, plane and glasspaper. It is a time consuming process but the rails will be always in view, so they need a good finish.

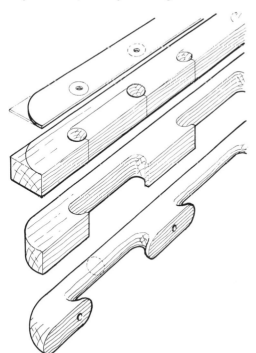

Fig 45 *Making hardwood grabrails.*

The counterbores for the fixing screws should be compatible with the pellet sizes and not more than $\frac{1}{2}$in deep. Drill the fixing holes through at clearance size and varnish the rails before fitting. When the rails are fitted, smear some glue into each counterbore before tapping the pellet home. Clean off the pellet with a chisel and sand it down flush with the rail. Finally, varnish the whole assembly.

Cockpit seats

The seating surfaces including the locker tops are sometimes moulded with an indented pattern to afford better grip when wet. If this is not so, they are usually finished with hardwood facing slats. These are about $\frac{1}{2}$in $\times$ 2in section with well rounded edges and ends. They are best spaced about $\frac{1}{2}$in to $\frac{3}{4}$in apart and will need a mastic bedding. The most simple method of fastening is by self tapping screws, counterbored $\frac{1}{4}$in deep followed by pellets. Alternatively, if the cockpit moulding is single skinned, brass wood-screws can be used from the underside into the slats. This method has the advantage that no sign of the fastenings can be seen from the outside, but it is a somewhat long-winded job requiring two pairs of hands.

It is an advantage to make the slats from teak or afrormosia so that varnishing is unnecessary. This will avoid the constant chore of cutting in the varnish work around the many edges, and result in a safer, non-slip finish.

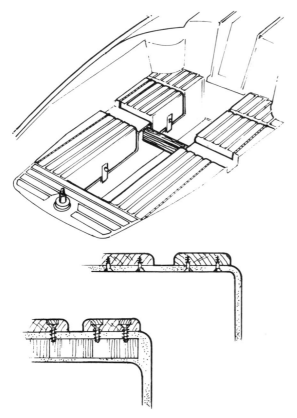

coachroof which requires no further work. Whilst these provide a reasonable non-slip surface it is difficult to achieve adequate penetration of the gel-coat into the mould without forming blow holes which appear on the finished moulding. Some moulders therefore prefer to produce smooth deck surfaces.

These must be overlaid by the builder with a suitable non-slip material. Really high quality, larger craft sometimes have a teak deck surface comprised of thin planking, bedded and laid over the fibreglass. This is most attractive but adds weight which the smaller craft cannot afford to carry, and of course adds considerably to the cost.

Most hulls with smooth decks are therefore fitted with a proprietary non-slip material. This is cork-like in texture with a flat, diamond scored face, supplied in sheets about 4ft × 3ft and attached to the deck with a special adhesive. It is advisable to lay the material in panels with a gap of $\frac{1}{2}$in to $\frac{3}{4}$in between each, rather than attempt tight butt joints which may eventually pull apart if shrinkage occurs.

Start the marking out process at the widest part of the deck, first ensuring that the panel length will work out acceptably along the deck length. Lay the material on the deck and mark it out with a fibrepen. Then lay the sheet on a suitable flat board and cut out the panel required using a sharp bench knife. Round off the corners by scoring around a small tin lid or something similar which is about 2in to 3in diameter. As each panel is cut, lay it dry on

Fig 46 *Cockpit seat slats. Inset shows alternative method of fixing to single or double skinned mouldings.*

Deck surfaces

Many manufacturers produce craft that have a diamond pattern moulded on to the deck and

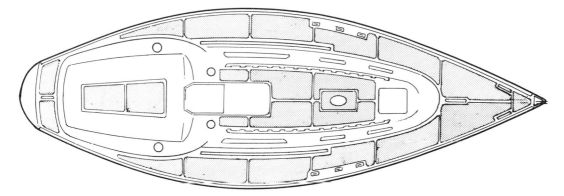

Fig 47 *Laying non-slip deck covering panels. Note the alignment of the deck and coachroof panels.*

the deck, and continue making the next panel until all of them are cut and laid out satisfactorily in the correct positions. Then carefully mark around each one with a wax crayon or chinagraph pencil and afterwards remove the panels.

The glossy face of the gel-coat must be roughened slightly where the panels are to fit in order to provide an adequate key for the adhesive. This is done with a coarse sanding disc or a tungsten carbide disc. You must tackle this job very carefully to avoid scratching the deck outside of the lines. This is particularly awkward at the corners but can be done using the edge of the disc with some caution.

The adhesive is obtained from the manufacturers of the deck covering material. Mix only enough to lay a couple of panels at a time and apply it to the deck and the panels as recom-

mended, paying particular attention to the edges. Then position them on the deck. As the material is rather springy, you may need to apply some weights to them whilst the adhesive sets. For this you can use a multitude of tins of paint or anything handy. When the adhesive has just hardened off (this may be around 24 hours according to the temperature) remove any surplus adhesive from around the edges before it becomes too hard.

As a cheaper alternative, you may prefer to use a non-slip deck paint. Mark out the areas to be covered, mask all around the edges with tape and apply fibreglass self-etching primer. The coarse particles in the non-slip paint tend to settle to the bottom of the can, so it must be stirred thoroughly before, and regularly during, application. Then peel the masking tape away before the paint is fully dry to avoid lifting the paint edge from the deck.

Cockpit floor

This can be treated in the same manner as either the decks or the cockpit seat facings.

Mast supports

Many sailing craft have their masts mounted on, rather than through, the deck. The mast stands either in a hinged tabernacle or a heel cup fitting which is mounted on a strong hardwood bolster. This is to spread the weight and transmit it to the bulkheads inside the hull. The bolster must be of substantial section, particularly if the mast is not positioned directly over a bulkhead. It must carry not only the weight of the mast but also the boom, all rigging, sails, the downward force imparted by the rigging tension and the downward component of the windforce on the sailplan.

22

Tanks

Fuel and fresh water can be stored in metal tanks, custom-built fibreglass ones which are built into the boat, or flexible plastic tanks.

Stainless steel is the best material for metal tanks, because it is less inclined to affect the taste of the water in the way that galvanised steel does. As metal tanks are so expensive, many owners now prefer the cheaper alternative of either fibreglass or flexible plastic tanks. The flexible plastic containers are frequently advertised in the magazines and are obtainable in a variety of sizes. Because they are flexible they can be contained in almost any available space within the joinery.

As with fuel tanks, the quantity of water to be carried must be limited to suit the boat's ability to carry it without the trim or waterline level being unduly upset. Sailing craft in the 20-25ft range will not normally carry more than 10-15 gallons whilst some of the larger power boats can carry relatively large quantities. It is therefore safest to take notice of the designer's recommendation with regard to the volume, and if you must carry additional water, take it aboard in cans.

Fibreglass tanks can be built into the boat in a variety of places, but they are usually positioned under the saloon berths or under the cabin floor, as space permits. If your boat has keel bolts, it is not advisable to build a tank over them unless the lid provides adequate access because they may need tightening or removing at some future date. If two tanks are to be built on opposite sides of the boat, they

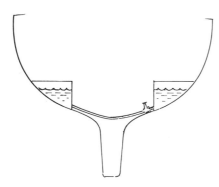

Fig 48 *Twin tanks joined by a balance pipe with a valve to prevent the contents from running to the lee side.*

should be linked by a balance pipe so that the water levels will equalise. On a sailing boat, the balance pipe must also be fitted with a valve which will be kept shut when sailing, to prevent all the water from running into the leeward tank.

The tank can be built directly on to the hull in the chosen position using plywood formers so that part of it is formed by the hull itself. This provides maximum capacity within a limited space and also helps to stiffen the hull. Cut the plywood sides and ends, and edge them around their tops with $\frac{3}{4}$in square timber, well rounded off. This will form the flange to which the top of the tank will be attached.

Set the panels up and attach them to the hull with resin putty or filler and when this is set, bond three layers of fibreglass over the whole assembly, inside and out. Also, overlap the hull by about 3in all round both inside

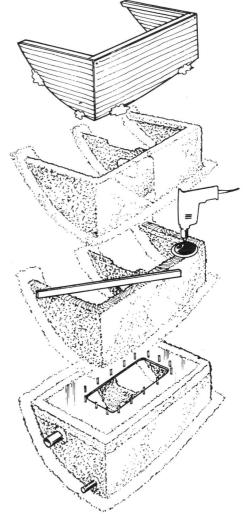

Fig. 49 *Making a fibreglass tank over ply formwork.*

and out and make sure that the fibreglass is neatly bonded around the top flanges.

If the tank is more than about 3ft long, make up a baffle in plywood. This should be a loose fit inside the tank to allow for the edge bonding and will require plenty of openings to allow the water to flow through. Bond over both sides, making sure that the edges of the holes and around the outside are well covered. When the fibreglass has cured, trim and fit the baffle, and using the same technique as the sides, bond it into position.

The filler and outlet tubes are usually fitted to the end of the tank to allow the pipework to run fairly under the floorboards or bunk top. These are best made from tube which is compatible in size with the deck filler cap fitting and tap connections, usually $1\frac{1}{2}$in and $\frac{1}{2}$in outside diameter respectively. They need be only about 3in or 4in long with a broad flange brazed round them, about 1in from the end. Bore holes in the end of the tank to suit the tubes, coat the underside of each flange with resin putty, place them in position and bond over the flanges. The position of the outlet tube must obviously be at the bottom of the tank end, or a plastic tube must be fitted to it inside the tank, to reach the bottom.

Clean off the top flange of the tank with a disc cutter and check across it with a straight edge as you proceed, to ensure that it is flat. Now clean any odd bits of fibreglass from the inside and paint it out thoroughly with gel-coat to ensure a complete seal of the fibreglass and also

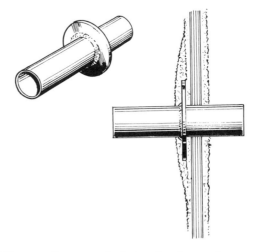

Fig 50a *Custom made fittings for the attachment of tubing to fibreglass tanks.*

provide a clean, smooth surface. Do not gel-coat the top of the flanged edges or the outside at this stage.

The top and its access cover are best made from a sheet of plain fibreglass about $\frac{3}{16}$in to $\frac{1}{4}$in thick. The cover is necessary to enable the tank to be opened occasionally for cleaning out. It must be large enough to allow access to all parts of the tank, and also to the keelbolts, if the tank is on the centreline. Therefore, if baffles are fitted, the opening must reach beyond them.

To laminate the flat sheets of fibreglass required, lay a piece of polythene sheet smoothly over a good, flat surface such as a piece of plywood and fix it to the edges with drawing pins. Cut about eight pieces of chopped strand mat to the size required to make both the tank top and the access cover. Now coat the face of the polythene sheet with resin and lay out the first laminate. Stipple the resin through and continue laminating until the required thickness is achieved. When the resin has cured, remove the resultant fibreglass panels from the poly-thene surface. You will see that the lower face is smooth and flat, so for the tank top this will be fitted uppermost, because it will provide the best seating face for the gasket. Trim the edges of the top to suit the tank, then mark the access opening. This should be about 1in smaller all round than the cover.

Trim the cover to size and mark the fixing screw positions $\frac{1}{2}$in from the edge at about 2in pitch. The screws will be $\frac{1}{4}$in diameter, so make slack clearance holes through the cover about $\frac{5}{16}$in diameter. Position the cover over the top access hole with its smooth face *downwards* and using it as a drill jig, spot the centres of the fixing holes with the clearance drill. Now, using a core size drill, drill through the top and thread the holes to suit the fixing screws. Fit the screws from the rough (inside) face of the top and bond over their heads to lock them.

The tank top, complete with its cover bolts, can now be fitted. Coat the tank flange tops with resin filler, bed the top into it and bond over the top and sides. Before the filler cures, reach into the tank and wipe around the join to smooth it over. When all is secure, paint the inside face of the top and the join with gel-coat.

A gasket will be required between the cover and the top. Use a strip of soft rubber and fix it with contact adhesive to the top between the line of bolts and the edge of the opening. Fit the cover over the screws with its smooth face underneath to form a good joint. Then fit a washer over each screw and tighten the lid down evenly all round with the nuts–preferably wing nuts.

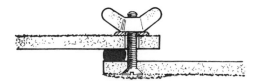

Fig 50b   *Tank lid: note the gasket positioned inside the screw line.*

23
Joinery

Before starting the internal joinery, ensure that the hull is still horizontal in both directions, so that the spirit level and plumb bob can be used when fitting and adjusting the furniture panels.

The most logical starting point is making the floors. These are the timbers that run across the bottom of the hull to strengthen it and also support the floor boards. The floors should be made of hardwood about $1\frac{1}{2}$in thick, shaped to suit the section of the hull and spaced at about 24in centres. Start in the forward end of the main cabin by fitting a floorboard support strut, about $1\frac{1}{4}$in square, across the aft face of the bulkhead. This will be the datum level for the floor, so set out the headroom dimension required at the bulkhead. Don't forget to make allowance for the headlining and the floorboard thickness. Now cut a template to make a floor (bearer) at the aft end. Using the template, cut the floor and fit it in position, trimming with a chisel and plane until it fits into the hull. When this is complete, cut generous limber holes to allow bilge water to pass through. Now trim the top edge until it lies horizontal across the hull and is also in horizontal alignment with the floor support on the bulkhead, checking with straight edge and spirit level.

When you are satisfied with the alignment, remove the floor and cross-score the sides ready for bonding. Apply a coat of resin filler to the bottom edge and press the floor down firmly into position and re-check the alignment. When this has set, cut and fit the two boards which form the fixed outer edges of the floor. These are best rebated to restrict the amount of dirt that can get into the bilge. Screw the boards into position and then, using the same technique as before, make and fit the intermediate floors using the boards as your level datum.

After all the floors are set up in alignment, prime their sides with resin and bond them to the hull using a minimum of three layers of chopped strand mat bonded over their full depth and running about 4in wide around the hull. You can now lay boards across the floors so that you have a sound, flat surface from which to work.

Bulkhead facings

If the bulkheads are to be covered with thin ply or laminated plastic to give a decorative finish and cover the bonded flanges, it should be tackled before any further panels are fitted. The templates used for making the bulkheads can be used for marking the panels out, but they may need slight adjustment. See how they lay over the bulkhead faces and make any improvement that may be required. The bonded flanges will probably form a step on the bulkhead faces and there may be odd bits of fibreglass sticking out. These must all be ground back to form a fair curvature to enable the facings to be glued over the entire face of the bulkhead and flanges. If using thin ply, chamfer all around the back face so that the edges will fit up close into the corners.

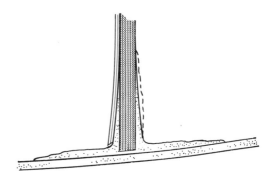

Fig 51   *Fitting bulkhead facing ply. The bonded flanges have been ground back to enable the facing to lie fair.*

The facings will be attached with contact adhesive. This gives an instant bond and thereby eliminates the necessity for clamps and pins. You must therefore locate the facing accurately before final contact. Application of the adhesive from its tin to the face of the bulkhead is somewhat awkward, so decant it into a squeezy bottle. You may need to enlarge the hole in the cap slightly, but this device will enable you to get the adhesive on to the face without making a mess.

When the facings are attached, re-cut the small access doorways as mentioned in the section on bulkheads, but leave the final cutting to size until later. This will avoid damage to the edges during the course of the general joinery work.

General layout

Accommodation drawings normally show just about the maximum number of berths, galley and toilet space etc that can be built into any given hull. However, you may wish to depart from the design in order to enlarge the galley or toilet at the expense of some other feature, or perhaps include a dinette instead of the traditional berth at each side of the cabin. Proposed alterations of this sort should be laid out to scale on an overtrace of the drawing so that all the dimensions and implications can be considered before work starts. If you refer only to the plan view, it is easy to be misled into the impression that you have more space than there really is. As you are working in three dimensions, any redesigning must be worked out with regard to the plan, elevation and the cross section shapes in order to take the compound curvature of the hull into account. Remember that you may wish to sell the craft at a later date, so do not build the accommodation to some peculiar whim which could make this difficult. The following dimensions give a general guide, but they will obviously be affected by the hull design.

Headroom:	6ft minimum, at least over part of the accommodation.
Settee berths:	6ft 2in minimum length × 22in to 24in wide × 14in to 18in from floor to cushion top. You should decide at this stage what thickness the squabs are to be, as this affects the joinery. 3in is adequate for berths, but if they are also to be used as seats, it is better to have them 4in thick.
Focsle berths:	6ft 6in minimum length where two meet. 24in wide at head end if possible.
Quarter berths:	6ft 2in minimum length × 22in to 24in wide at head × 9in wide at foot.
WC compartment:	24in minimum measured across the WC × 16in minimum space in front × 18in from floor to seat level.

If a dinette style layout is to be incorporated, the floor and seat levels may have to be raised above the main floor in sailing craft, in order to

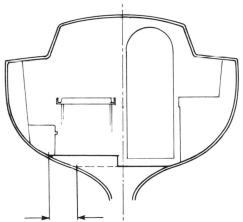

Fig 52 *Dinette accommodation. In a sailing craft it is usually necessary to raise the floor level under the dinette to achieve additional width.*

gain sufficient width (see fig 52). As the dinette is designed to convert into a double berth, its minimum squab width is about 3ft 6in. Taking hull section shape into account, this means that they are not a practical proposition in boats with less than about 9ft beam.

Fig 53 *General arrangement of a typical dinette. Compare with Fig 52 to see difference between a two- and three-dimensional visualisation of the layout.*

Internal mast support blocks

In sailing craft with through-deck masts, the mast heel fitting stands on a solid block, bonded to the inside of the hull, usually directly over the keel. The height of the block must be correct if a standard mast and rigging set is to be used or the rigging will not fit. The critical dimension is from the top face of the block to the top face of the coachroof where the mast emerges.

The block itself can be either solid or laminated hardwood with scored sides bedded on resin putty and bonded into place. To find its position, mark out the position of the mast centre on deck and drill a small reference hole through at this point. Using the hole to locate the plumb bob cord, the plumb bob will indicate the position vertically below it and this will be at the centre of the block if the mast is to be vertical. If the design indicates that the mast is to be raked, then the position required to achieve the rake can be set out using the bob as a vertical datum. It is important to get the mast in the right position and at the correct angle initially, although many heel fittings allow the angle to be adjusted slightly in a fore and aft direction. This is so that the sailing performance can be tuned later on.

If keelbolts are positioned within its base area, cut-outs large enough for a box spanner must give access to them. They may need tightening at some future date. The top part of the block can be made detachable in this case so that the cut-outs are covered in.

The panel supports

In each of the compartments, the transverse
bulkheads, which have been fitted earlier, form
the datum points from which all the joinery
is set out. The first panels to be fitted will be
attached to them, and then the work progresses
from there.

Mark out the positions where back and bunk
front panels are to fit against the bulkheads.
The marks should indicate where the back face
of the panel fits, so you must make allowance
for its thickness and screw 1in square timber
supports to the bulkhead along these lines. If the
panels arc to run obliquely to the bulkheads,
the front faces of the supports will require a
bevel to allow the panels to lay flat against them.
To determine this, lay a straight edge across the
supports at each end and bevel them until it
lays fair.

Dividing webs

These are fitted behind the larger panels to support them and also stiffen the hull and form
divisions to the lockers. They must be fitted
before the panels so templates must be cut to
fit the hull and the straight edge used to align
their front edges with the other supports. When
they have been cut and fitted satisfactorily,
glue and pin a 1in square timber alongside the
front edge to form an attachment flange for the
panel (see fig 54). Set them up in their posi-

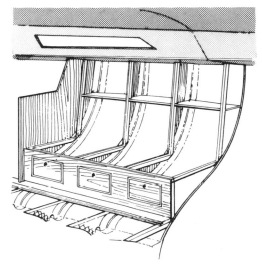

Fig 54 *Webs and shelves. These must all be fitted
before the panel templates are made.*

tions in resin filler and check the front edge
alignment. Then bond them to the hull after the
filler has cured.

The panels

Modern boats are fitted out almost entirely
with plywood panels. These form all the shelves,
locker and bunk fronts, galley focsle and toilet
compartment joinery. They are between $\frac{3}{8}$in to
$\frac{1}{2}$in thick, depending on the size of craft, and
usually have a decorative face veneer. The panels
themselves are either bonded to the hull, joined

to the bulkheads or to each other to form a self-supporting structure which imparts additional strength to the hull.

When all the supports are fitted, make cardboard templates for the panels required. These will be cut to lay against the supports, and also follow along under the deck or around the contour of the hull as required. The templates indicate the shape of the *back* face of the panels so when you use them to mark out the plywood sheets, do not forget to make generous allowance for the bevels required.

Offer each panel to its position and note which edges require bevelling. Remove the panel, bevel the edges with a plane and try it in position again. This is a laborious job until you become skilled, but there are no short cuts. Just a little bit too much planed off, or the bevel running the wrong way, and you have an unsightly gap where there should be a nice, tight butt joint. This is most important at the ends where the panels meet the bulkheads. Under the decks, the top edges are usually covered by the head linings, whilst along the hull, a clearance fit is preferable for bonding.

Locker doors etc

With the blank panels in place, mark out the positions of the locker openings and pigeon holes, and attach the timber supports for the bunk top panels. These must all be set out with reference to the horizontal by means of spirit level and straight edge. Now the panels can be removed and taken back to the workshop for cutting and finishing. All the doors, doorstops, catches and shelf supports should now be completed before the panels are finally fitted into the boat.

With careful cutting, the locker doors can be made with the pieces cut from the panels. This economises on plywood usage and also means that the decorative veneer faces retain a continuity of grain on the finished assembly. To achieve this, a series of small holes (about $\frac{1}{16}$in diameter) drilled close together along each edge line of the proposed openings will allow you to push your jigsaw blade through in order to cut the door out with no wastage. When the openings have been cut, clean them out with a coarse file in order to straighten the edges. The type of door that is quickest to make has generously radiused (about $1\frac{1}{2}$in) corners. These entail making only one jigsaw insertion for each door.

You must decide what style of edge finishing that you will use for all the openings and locker door edges and use it as your standard throughout the boat. The simplest way is to veneer the edges of both the openings and the doors. Suitable veneers to match the panel faces can be purchased at your local 'Do-it-yourself' shop. These can be cut with a sharp bench knife as required and attached with contact adhesive. It can be applied very conveniently with a squeeze container as previously described. Deal first with the openings and then trim the doors down to size with a plane, making allowance for the door

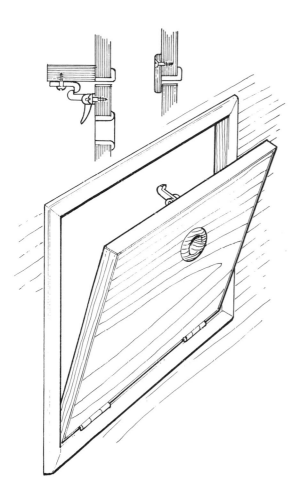

Fig 55 *Locker doors. A high quality finish achieved by edging the openings and veneering the door edges.*

edge veneering plus a $\frac{1}{16}$in finished clearance all round.

If you prefer rectangular openings, a high quality appearance is afforded by edging them with a matching timber moulding. These can be cut on the sawbench in long strips (see fig 55). Round off the edges with a plane and glass-paper block and fit them with 45° mitred corners. Veneer the edges of the doors.

Hinges These require rebates in both the door and the panel edge to make a neat fit allowing about $\frac{1}{16}$in clearance along the hinge edge. The normal domestic brass hinges have steel pins, which quickly rust and break if used on a boat, so you must buy marine hinges with brass pins from a ship's chandler.

Stops On the opposite side to the hinges, fit small stops for the doors to close against. These need be only about $\frac{3}{4}$in $\times$ $\frac{1}{4}$in section, cut from any hardwood then glued and pinned to the back face of the panel, overlapping the opening by about $\frac{1}{4}$in.

Catches These must be of the spring latch type. Ball catches are not suitable because the gear stored in the cupboards will burst the doors open when the boat rolls. Again, the catches must be of all brass construction. The most popular type is a simple open latch with a finger lever. They are operated through a finger hole in the door which is finished with a glued-in teak bullseye (see fig 55).

Shelf support battens can now be glued and pinned to the back face of the panels. These will be referenced parallel to the locker doors and should just about complete all of the detail required. The panels can now be varnished (two coats both sides) before finally being fitted and fastened. If any further bonding or glue joints are to be made when fitting, the plywood face should be left unvarnished in the required area.

The panels can now be glued and pinned in position on the supports and webs. You will have to drill a pilot hole through the panel into the supports in order to drive the brass panel pins. Then, with a small punch, tap the heads just below the face of the panels and stop the holes in with matching filler.

Berth front panels

These are similar to the other panels, fitted with locker doors etc, as required. To retain the berth cushions, make them 2in to 3in higher than the berth top level and fit a capping piece along the top edges (see fig 56).

Berth tops

These can be dealt with in several ways, the simplest being just loose plywood panels, about $\frac{3}{8}$in thick, which rest on support struts attached to the joinery. To keep the panels a convenient size, each berth top should be divided into at

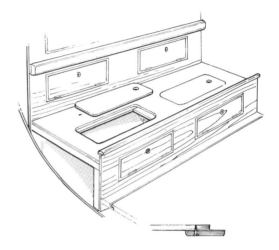

Fig 56 *Berth tops. Structural strength is gained by making fixed tops with small lids.*

least two parts, the dividing line being positioned to coincide with a web or a support beam. A 1in diameter hole near the end of each panel will facilitate lifting. This method provides maximum access for storage in the bilge area beneath the berths.

A better quality job, giving greater rigidity to the structure, can be made by fitting fixed tops with smaller, removeable hatches. These hatches can have corners of about 1in radius and can be cut in the same manner as the locker doors. Strips of plywood, about 2in wide, glued and screwed to the underside of the top can be fitted so that a land, about $\frac{3}{8}$in wide, is created for the hatches to rest on.

Floorboards

These need to be at least $\frac{3}{4}$in thick ply to take the weight of a person standing on them at a point midway between the floors, without undue flexing. To make a neat job, finish the sides with a broad hardwood strip, rebated to overlap the fixed floor side members. They should be fitted to about $\frac{1}{16}$in clearance all round to prevent jamming and each one requires a flush lifting ring at one end.

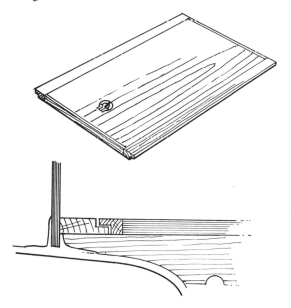

Fig 57   *Floor boards with rebated edges to prevent dirt falling into the bilges.*

24
The Galley

The two key facilities in any galley are the stove and the sink, with its water supply and drainage arrangements. With these two items at hand, you must decide how they are to fit into the space available, and also provide adequate work tops, cupboards for food and utensils, plus at least one drawer for the cutlery.

It is normal to position the stove parallel with the centreline of the boat so that it can be gimballed fore and aft. This gives a relatively horizontal surface for the kettle or saucepans when the boat rolls or heels. Adequate space must therefore be provided underneath and at the back of the stove to allow for this movement. A variety of stoves are available, fuelled by bottled gas, paraffin (kerosene), and alcohol (methylated spirit), with or without grills or ovens. Alcohol stoves usually have integral fuel tanks, but paraffin and gas-fuelled stoves normally have their fuel supplies mounted in tanks remote from the stove.

Paraffin stoves work on the pressure principle; the burners are supplied with fuel from a pressurised tank which is mounted within the joinery, close to the stove. Fuel pressure is generated by a hand pump mounted either directly on the side of the tank or nearby and connected to it by a pipe. Connection between the tank and the stove is by means of a flexible high pressure pipe which allows the stove to swing freely in its gimbals.

Many people prefer to use bottled gas appliances, because they are thought to be more clean, quick and controllable. It is, however, probably

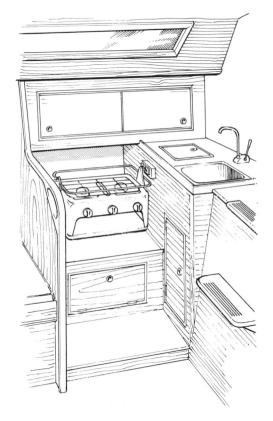

Fig 58 *General arrangement of the galley area. Note the clearance required behind and underneath the stove.*

the most dangerous fuel, because it is highly explosive and also toxic. You must never forget that it is heavier than air, so any leakage will settle into the boat's bilges. Here it could be ignited accidentally by any spark, or it could

build up and poison the occupants. The engine or a match could cause an explosion severe enough to burst the whole boat apart, so *always turn the gas off at the bottle after use*. The bottle and regulator should be mounted in a gas tight locker, preferably in the cockpit. The locker bottom must be above the waterline and have a drain to lead any loose gas overboard. The feed pipe must be all metal to a point just short of the stove. Here it joins to a length of armoured flexible pipe with an approved gas proof rubber lining which connects to the stove. This pipe must allow the stove to swing freely in its gimbals. The gimbals are normally incorporated in the fiddle surround and are hung in sockets attached to the adjacent joinery.

When choosing your sink, bear in mind your limited water supply and the possible difficulties of restraining cooks from reckless wastage. Large sinks require the use of more water. Also, beware of the round, tapered bowl type. Some of them are a perfect jamming fit for the average dinner plate and once in this predicament, the only way to retrieve the plate is to disconnect the drain pipe and poke the plate out from underneath, so the small square sinks are the best.

The drain pipe outlet fitting should be sited just above the boat's waterline. This means that the sink outlet must be at least 6in above this level, or a sink drain pump must be fitted.

When you have decided on the layout, make a template of the front panel and mark out the positions of the drawer and cupboard openings.

Using the same techniques as the other panels, make and fit the complete assembly with doors, shelf supports etc. The stove bay should be at least 2in longer than the stove to allow room for cleaning.

Now the panels which form the sides of the stove bay can be fitted. These will be joined to the front and also bonded to the hull to form a division to the cupboards. They will also have shelf supports in alignment with those on the back of the front panel and supports for both the bottom and the back of the stove bay.

The bottom of the bay can also run right out to the boat's side to form the bottom of a bin-type locker behind the stove. This utilises otherwise unusable space. When it has been fitted, remove it and cover its top face with laminated plastic before fixing it into place. Now the back panel can be fitted and covered in the same manner. Cover the bay sides in laminated plastic, and before any more joinery is fitted, install the pipework for the sink drain, gas and water supplies.

The drawer and its runner assembly can now be made. The drawer itself should be a good clearance fit through its opening. Make the sides and ends in hardwood or ply about $\frac{1}{2}$in thick with simple half-lap corner joints. Groove the bottom inside faces about $\frac{5}{16}$in from the bottom to suit the bottom panel. The front, which has been cut from the galley front panel is best attached to the front of the drawer assembly in the form of a fascia, rather than be an integral part of it (see fig 59). If the drawer is to contain

cutlery, fit a set of partitions to make at least five bays as shown.

The runners are best made up as an integral assembly for attachment to the other joinery. In

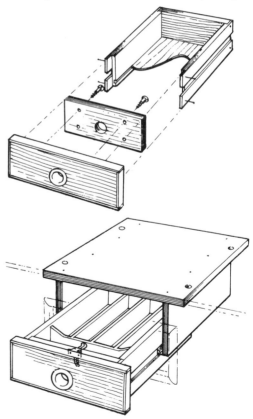

Fig 59 *Drawer construction. The slide assembly is built independently from the other joinery to make fitting easier.*

this way they can be made on the bench to fit the drawer accurately. The assembly can be designed to attach to either the front panel or the underface of the unit top.

Now fit all the internal shelves and the unit top. These can all be plastic covered before final attachment and if you have made a bin locker behind the stove, a hatch will be needed. A fiddle capping around all the exposed edges of the top and stove bay will give a neat finish.

When the drawer runner assembly is fitted, ensure that the drawer runs freely, and offer the fascia up to it. Note carefully its position and attach it with screws from the inside of the drawer. Fit wooden stops to the runners to prevent the drawer from running too far. Finally, fit a catch similar to the locker catches, to stop the drawer from ejecting itself when the boat rolls.

25

The Toilet Compartment

The main problem here is obviously the successful installation of a suitable WC. There are a number of different types available ranging from the simple chemical container to the sea water flushing variety. If the craft is to be used on inland waterways, canals or lakes, chemical toilets are usually obligatory, but for seagoing, flushing toilets are preferable. These have separate inlet and outlet fittings through the hull, a pump (or possibly two) and the necessary pipework. The makers' installation instructions always give sketches and recommendations and these should be followed closely when arranging the layout. The valves fitted to the inlet and outlet skin fittings must be easily accessible because they must always be turned off when leaving the boat. The inlet must be sited forward of the outlet and the outlet pipe must be arched up from the WC well above the waterline before descending again to the skinfitting.

Taking these requirements into account, you must sort out just where everything has to fit. The toilets are only about 9in high from the base to the seat level so they need to be mounted on a strong shelf or plinth to bring the height to about 16in from floor to seat level. In some craft, the pump can be mounted under the focsle berth with only the handle protruding through a slot into the WC compartment. This saves valuable space and also enables the pipework to be run out of sight behind the focsle panelling to the skin fitting situated under the focsle berth.

It is preferable to cover the bulkhead faces

In smaller boats where, through lack of space, the WC has to be installed facing the centreline, there is usually room to fit a cupboard under the sidedeck, but not a fixed washbasin. In this case, it is often possible to build the sink on runners so that it stows neatly away under the cupboard when the loo is in use. The runners are attached to the bulkhead at either side of the compartment so that, to use the sink, it is pulled out over the loo. This arrangement avoids the

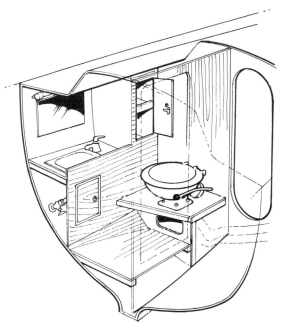

Fig 60 *The toilet compartment. The WC pipework can be run through the bulkhead to hull valves under the focsle berth.*

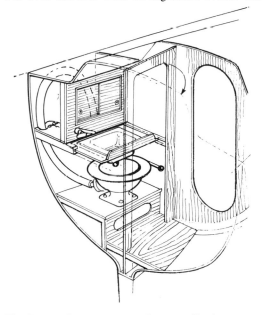

Fig 61 *Toilet compartment for a smaller boat showing a slide away sink. The door is arranged so that it closes off the saloon and thereby gives more room in the toilet.*

with laminated plastic, so this is the first part of the job. The joinery will be similar in concept to that of the galley, so many of the same operations are involved. It consists of a unit which includes a small washbasin, water supply, drainage and cupboard underneath. As in the galley, the unit top and also the WC plinth should be plastic covered. You must be careful when arranging the layout to ensure that the cupboard door will clear the front of the WC.

need for the drainpipe, valve and skin fitting
because the sink can drain directly into the WC
(see fig 61). The WC door can be arranged so
that it either closes the toilet compartment or
divides the saloon from the focsle (fig 61).

Mast support systems

Sailing craft with deck stepped masts tend to
need an arrangement whereby the bulkheads
forming the WC compartment and the oilskin
hanging locker opposite also support the mast.
Extra strength is built in by means of beams to
reinforce the bulkheads over the doorways and
vertical struts lodged under them which also
form the sides to the doorways. These beams
and struts are glued and screwed to the bulkheads and their purpose is to transfer the load
from the mast bolster on deck to the hull.

Doorways

These can now be cut to shape and finished
off. Because of the curvature of the coachroof
and the necessity to retain strength at the top
of the bulkhead, the head of the doorway is
often required to be semi-circular in shape. This
means that it will not be practical to edge it
with a solid timber moulding so, to cover the
plywood edges, you can fit either a veneered or
a light, laminated timber surround. The bottom,
which will have to withstand a lot of wear,
should be fitted with a solid timber step.

26
The Focsle

The joinery here is fairly simple, consisting usually of a forepeak locker and two berths with lockers underneath. Some amateur builders prefer to start their joinery here so that they can develop skills in the art of fixing oblique panels and so on, in less of a showcase area than the main cabin. Another advantage is that it is easier to fit out the relatively confined focsle using the as yet empty cabin as your 'workshop'. This reduces the chance of accidental damage to the finished work.

The forepeak locker is formed by a small triangular bulkhead which strengthens the bow and squares off the forward end of the focsle. It is bonded into position in the normal way and has a small, lift-off hatch cut through for access. In some craft, particularly those with bluff bow sections, this locker is used for anchor chain storage via a chain pipe fitting on deck, but it is better to keep the chain further aft.

The focsle is usually divided by a low bulkhead, forward of which the two berths are joined. Its top edge forms a support for the berth tops so if you make and fit this bulkhead first, you have a convenient datum from which to set out the rest of the work. Fit a 1in square beading to the forward top edge and ensure that this is set up horizontal before bonding it into the hull.

Using the straight edge and level, mark out and attach horizontal berth support beadings to the forepeak bulkhead and the after focsle bulkhead. Now, mark out the positions for the two berth front panels and attach support beadings to the two bulkheads, ready to receive them.

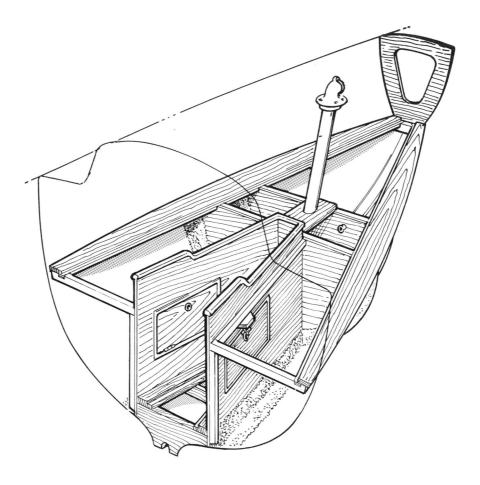

Fig 62 *A typical focsle. Loose ply lids are used to form the base for the upholstered cushions.*

To support the berth tops along the hull sides, make and fit boards which rest on the bulkhead and the two end supports. These should be about $\frac{3}{4}$in thick and their width will be determined by the amount of curvature in the hull because their outside edges must be cut to fit around this curve. They require a support lip made from $\frac{1}{2}$in $\times$ 2in strips of ply, overlapping the inboard edges by about $\frac{1}{2}$in and running their full length. These are to support the berth tops, and they can be notched out to clear the bulkhead and the end supports. When the assemblies fit satisfactorily, glue and pin them in position on the structure and bond the boards to the hull along their length, top and bottom. These also help to strengthen the bow section.

Cut and fit the berth front panels in the normal way, including the locker doors, catches, shelf and berth supports etc. Make the panels 2in to 3in higher than the berth top level to retain the berth cushions. At the forward end, a make up piece on the top of the bulkhead will be required to bring it level and then fit a hardwood capping all round. Once the general structure is complete, decide how you intend to divide the top panels. If there are any large areas (above about 18in square) left unsupported, extra beams will be required. These can simply be fitted and glued under the side supports and their ends bonded to the hull.

Chain locker

Many sailing craft have rather fine bow sections which, if they are to carry anchor chain as opposed to warp, demand that the chain is carried well away from the bow in order to reduce their tendency to pitch when at sea. Therefore the chain is usually carried immediately forward of the low bulkhead that we have just discussed. To create a secure chain locker, another similar bulkhead is required, about 18in further forward. Bridging the space between the two, a timber about 6in $\times \frac{3}{4}$in section is fitted. This is bored and recessed to support the lower end of a piece of 2in plastic pipe which is fitted under the hawse pipe fitting on deck. Here it is bonded to the underside of the deck with a collar of fibreglass. This pipe guides the chain into the locker with no risk of the cabin being soiled by mud and water. It also provides an adequate drop from the lower end of the pipe to the bottom of the locker. This fall is essential, otherwise as the chain is fed into the locker, it will pile up to the pipe and not allow any more in. A stout ringbolt should be fitted near the top of the forward chain locker bulkhead for seizing the end of the chain.

In the type of smaller craft which have a WC installed in the focsle, the berths, in the form of pipecots, are made to hinge up clear of the WC. In this case the joinery here is usually confined to the forepeak bulkhead, a low bulkhead immediately forward of the WC and open topped sail bins with slatted fronts.

27
Linings

When the joinery has been completed, large areas of unsightly bare fibreglass will still be left in view. Therefore, linings of one sort or another will be required to finish off the coach-roof, cabin sides, focsle, galley and inside the lockers. Some of the more expensive fibreglass craft are fitted with excellent moulded head-linings which cover the inside of the coachroof, cabin sides and, in some cases, part of the decks as well. These mouldings save a great deal of detailed work but, as with almost everything else, the rising costs have caused manufacturers to cut their specifications wherever possible in order to remain competitive. Therefore, most boats are now supplied as bare hulls and decks.

Linings can be made with a variety of facings according to your taste in decorative style but basically they fall into two categories: soft linings glued directly to the hull and hard backed or panel linings which can be made detachable.

Soft linings

Synthetic fabric materials can be glued with fabric adhesive directly to the hull to line lockers and cupboards. This gives a very much more finished appearance to the inside and also masks the translucent quality of the fibreglass hull. Some people are disturbed by the sight of sunlight shining through the hull and waves passing by.

Foam-backed vinyl is another good material. It has the advantage of being easily cleaned and can also be attached directly to fibreglass using contact adhesive. It is only necessary to apply one coat of adhesive to the fibreglass and then smooth the material on to it whilst it is still wet. It can be used with good effect on the coachroof sides, focsle sides, bulkheads etc. All these direct linings can be attached anywhere that has a reasonably smooth, fair surface. Therefore, before application of the adhesive, it is as well to check and remove any odd bumps or bits of mat or resin that may be sticking up within the area that is to be covered, or they will spoil the finished surface.

Panel linings

Some parts of the boat are not suitable for direct lining because the inside of the moulding is indented where winch bases, mast pads and other details are formed, or else there are stringers protruding so panel backed linings are necessary. In the instances where access behind is not required, such as coachroof side linings, the panels can be fixed. Others, such as headlinings, will need to be detachable to facilitate tightening or removal of bolt-on fittings such as winches, which may need workshop maintenance.

The panels are made of thin ply (about $\frac{1}{8}$in thick), either decorative veneered, or plain with foam-backed vinyl, laminated plastic or any other finished facing attached before assembly. Fixed panels can be attached directly to the

fibreglass by means of thick, fast mix, resin filler 'pancakes' daubed in strategic places on their backs. They are then quickly positioned and held in place with temporary struts whilst the cure takes place.

Detachable linings can be held in place with screws, screws and battens, or in some places can be sprung in around a curve between two bulkheads. This latter method is suitable for the focsle or quarter berth backs. Suitable anchorage points must be provided if they are to be screwed into place. These can be battens attached to the bulkheads, or battens attached to the hull or stringers with resin.

Headlinings

Some deck mouldings are of double skinned (unlined) construction with a balsa wood core. These are suitable for the attachment of headlinings with screws through the inner glass skin. (Don't forget the pilot holes.) As it is not possible to fit a headlining in one piece, they are usually divided longitudinally, preferably into three sections. To avoid the use of screws through the lining faces, the outboard edges can be lodged on beadings attached to the coachroof side lining. The inboard edges and the centre panel can then be neatly supported by two hardwood battens screwed to the deck moulding and running the length of the lining (see fig 63).

If foam-backed vinyl is used for panel cover-

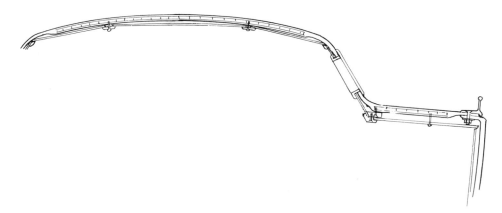

Fig 63   *Section showing removeable head linings and fixed panel linings to the coachroof sides. The linings along the inside of the hull can be sprung into place between the fixed joinery units.*

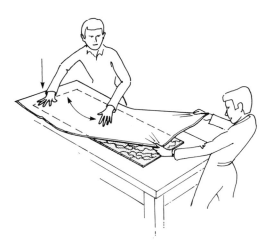

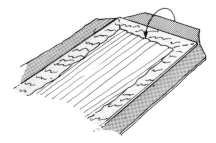

Fig 64   *Covering panel linings. The material is laid under light tension over wet contact adhesive. The edges are then stretched over and pressed on to the back.*

ings, in order to achieve a good finish it is important that it is drawn tightly across the panels and around the edges. To allow for this, the panels must be cut about $\frac{1}{8}$in undersize all round and then the vinyl covering cut to overlap the panel edge by about 3in all round. Coat the face of the panel with contact adhesive and, with the aid of an assistant, position the material onto the face while your assistant, still holding his end just clear of the panel, applies a steady pulling force. In this way, the material is kept under a light tension as you continue smoothing it on along the panel with the palms of your hands, making sure that there are no wrinkles as you go. Now, turn the panel over and apply a 3in band of adhesive all around the edges, cut mitres at the corners of the vinyl, stretch the overlap tightly over the edge and press it down. Panels covered in this manner have a relatively soft 'pillow' edge which assists them to accommodate minor irregularities and fit snugly into place.

28
Rudders and Steering Gear

The majority of sailing craft under 30ft are steered by means of a tiller. This simple device puts the helmsman in direct control of the rudder and enables him to feel so much about the boat's performance. Also, from his position well aft, he can keep a constant eye on the sailplan and wind direction.

On the other hand, some of the larger sailing craft and almost all power craft are steered by a wheel, situated well forward of the rudder. The wheel will operate the rudder via one of several systems. The most common ones are:

1 Pulleys and wires (see fig 65). A simple, cheap system. Old fashioned but still popular.

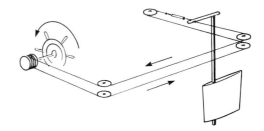

Fig 65

2 Morse control systems. The wheel operates a pinion engaged in a rack. This is connected to a tiller via a single, semi-flexible cable in a robust sheath. The sheath is fixed into the boat so that, as the wheel is turned, the rack pulls or pushes the cable through it and so moves the tiller (see fig 66). It is simple to install and reliable in service.

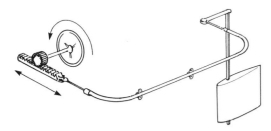

Fig 66

3 Hydraulic systems. The wheel is connected directly to a small vane pump which is in closed circuit via two pipes with a double acting cylinder, connected to the tiller. Turning the wheel therefore pumps the cylinder piston forward or backward, moving the tiller (see fig 67).

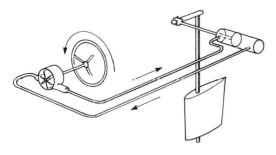

Fig 67

Power boat steering gear is often not easily accessible and the tillers are short. This means that, if a fault develops, hand steering may not be possible and the boat could be in trouble. It is therefore necessary to provide a means of operating the rudder direct if the need arises.

This is achieved by fitting an emergency tiller which can be made to locate on the rudder head or as an extension to the tiller itself, depending on the space available. If the steering gear were to jam, it would be necessary to disconnect it from the tiller in order to steer. Make sure that this can be done in a hurry, using only the tools that will always be carried on board.

Rudders

The size, shape and style of the rudder is an integral part of the hull design. This is particularly important in sailing craft because the rudder affects the geometric balance required between the hull and the sail plan. The rudder is invariably included within the purchase price of every hull and, at extra charge, the moulders are usually able to supply sets of suitable fittings. These are often designed to suit the particular rudder and hence are a good buy: standard fittings purchased elsewhere are not likely to be suitable in many cases.

There are three basic types of rudder, common to both power and sailing craft. These are transom, spade and skeg. They are made in fibreglass and are usually hollow with two halves bonded together. Spade and skeg hung rudders incorporate within their blades a stainless steel reinforcing frame, which is welded to a heavy stock made of stainless steel bar. The top or head of the stock is machined into a square tang which locates the rudder head (tiller) fitting.

Fitting transom hung rudders

These are hung on a set of four gudgeons through which a pintle bar is fitted and usually, a heel pintle at the bottom. The pintle bar and gudgeon assembly is arranged so that the rudder cannot be lifted off accidentally by the sea or by grounding. They are attached to the rudder with stainless steel screws, tapped into the fibreglass. The inside of the hull must be strengthened by means of stout timber or plywood pads, bedded in filler and heavily bonded over to

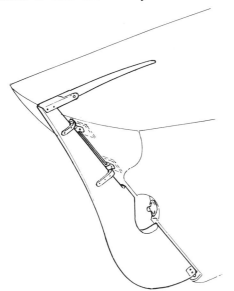

Fig 68   *Transom hung rudder. Note reinforcing pads inside the transom to spread the strain over a wider area.*

spread the strain transmitted from the transom gudgeons. The gudgeons must be attached with bolts passing through the transom and the pads, with nuts and washers fitted on the inside.

First, fit the heel pin and the gudgeons to the rudder. Then fit the heel socket to the hull and assemble the pintle bar and transom gudgeons to the rudder. The rudder can now be located in its heel socket and set up against the transom, on the centreline. Using the gudgeons as a drill guide, spot the hole positions on the transom, remove the rudder and drill the bolt holes. Coat the fitting faces with mastic and the assembly can be finally fitted.

Fitting spade rudders

The stock passes through a tube, set in the hull. It is fitted at each end with a bronze or plastic bearing and the top end terminates in a flange which is bolted through the deck moulding.

By measurement, mark the centre position of the tube on the outside of the hull and drill a $\frac{1}{8}$in diameter pilot hole. Then, by hanging a plumb bob over the hole inside the hull, you can mark a point on the underneath of the deck moulding which is directly above the hole and check that it is on the centreline by measurement to each side of the hull.

Most spade rudders are installed with the stock vertical so this mark will indicate the centre position where the tube is to penetrate the deck, and so this also can be pilot drilled. If not, the mark will be the datum from which you can set out any angle that may be required.

Using a hole cutter to suit the outside diameter of the tube, make a hole in both the deck moulding and the hull. Slide the tube into place, drill and tap through the deck for the flange bolts and also mark around the tube where it emerges underneath the hull. Remove the tube, cut off any surplus length, coat the flange face with mastic and refit it, pulling the flange down securely with the bolts. Now bond tightly around the tube at its top and bottom on the inside of the hull with at least five layers of 2oz mat. Remember that the bottom bonding must be watertight, so be careful to make a really neat job of the laminates, stippling out all the wrinkles and air.

To increase the strength of the area, stout plywood webs at each side and at the front and back of the tube are necessary. These also require heavy bonding. If, as is probable, the hull section is narrow at this point, it is a good plan to bond a plywood dam into place just forward of the tube. The dam should extend to just above the waterline level and be backfilled with a mix of mat offcuts in resin, similar to the technique described in the section on engine installations. This will create a solid block which will spread the strain out into the hull and also prevent leaks.

The rudder is retained in the tube by means of a collar which fits over the stock. This collar must be pre-drilled to suit a substantial

through bolt. With the rudder stock in position in the tube, fit the collar and seat it on the face of the flange. The through bolt position can then be transferred to the stock. Remove the rudder and drill the bolt hole. The rudder can now be fitted finally with the collar and bolt.

It is worth noting that most ordinary domestic electric drills are not powerful enough to drill holes much above $\frac{1}{4}$in diameter in stainless steel, and they also run much too fast. To drill this material successfully, you must use a speed reducing attachment. This will give more torque

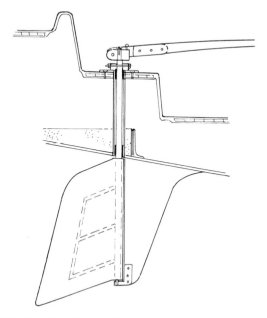

Fig 69 *Skeg hung rudder.*

and prevent the drill bit from burning out. You
must also use a very sharp, high speed steel drill
bit and apply heavy cutting pressure to make the
tool cut, rather than rub, into the material.

Fitting skeg rudders

These are similar in concept to spade rudders so
the same remarks apply except that the centre
position of the tube will be referenced from the
skeg and a heel fitting is used to link the rudder
to the foot of the skeg. This can be dealt with
after the rudder and tube have been fitted.

29

Masts, Spars and Rigging

Virtually all sailing craft now have extruded light alloy spars. They are made by a number of manufacturers to suit specific classes of boat. Hull manufacturers and agents are usually able to supply the spars complete with sets of rigging. These should all fit together without problems, providing that you have the mast heel fitting in the correct position in relation to the stem, backstay and shroud fittings.

Alternatively, some companies offer spar kits. You have to specify the size and type of craft and they will then supply the extrusions and all the necessary fittings loose. The fittings are attached with 'pop' rivets of various sizes, applied with a special rivet gun which is often obtainable on hire from the same company. A booklet will normally be supplied with the kit which gives tips on the method of assembly.

There are two main difficulties for the amateur tackling his own rigging at home. They are the availability of a hydraulic swaging press and the problem of erecting the mast to ascertain the correct lengths of the wires. If the mast is over about 25ft long and is not deck mounted in a hinged tabernacle, you will need either a crane or high sheer legs to erect it safely.

However, if you do intend to make your own standing rigging, consult the sailplan to find the various sizes of wire required. Most favoured is stainless steel in 1×19 construction, non-flexible wire. The designers rarely give specific details of the lengths required because there are many end fitting arrangements and turnbuckles available. This means that you will have to sort out

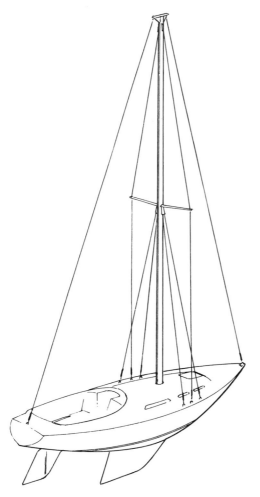

Fig 70 *Typical standing rigging system comprising of forestay, backstay, cap shrouds, foreward and aft lower shrouds.*

all these details yourself, allowing about 6in extra length for each eyesplice.

With the complete mast and all the turnbuckles at hand, cut the wires to length and make the eyesplices at one end of each wire. If you have no splicing press available, you will have to get them done by a chandler or rigger. Do not forget that each eye must be formed around a stainless steel thimble.

The eyes can then be attached to their correct positions on the mast. Erect the mast and secure it in the vertical position with three temporary rope guys. Unscrew each turnbuckle to about three-quarters of its range and attach it to its eyeplate on deck. The rigging wires can now be gauged off against each one and, by bending and taping the wire back on itself, the position of the lower eyes will be determined. Lower the mast again and all the remaining eyesplices can be completed.

The halliards are relatively simple to organise because their lengths can be measured directly from the mast. Many cruising boats use pre-stretched synthetic fibre rope, in which case a simple eye splice with a thimble at the top end and a whipping at the other does the job adequately. Racing boats and larger craft have halliards of galvanised flexible steel wire with rope tails. If you are an expert rigger, capable of making the necessary wire to rope splice, you will not be reading this section anyway. If not, just measure off the distance between the sheaves and note the other details to give to a rigger so that he can make the halliards for you.

30

Paints and Finishes

In order to withstand the cumulative damaging effects of sea, sun, rain and cold, all the external finishes must be of marine quality, applied in the manner specified by their manufacturers. It is therefore well worth obtaining a copy of one of the various booklets on the application of marine finishes from your chandler. There are however, certain pointers that can be borne in mind in conjunction with the booklets.

The hull

Some people are under the impression that fibreglass boats never need paint of any sort. This is, of course, a mistake even with a brand new boat, because the underwater part must be thoroughly coated with an antifouling paint to hinder the growth of weed and barnacles.

The first job to be done is to mark the waterline, and mask the hull above it with tape. Most hulls already have the waterline moulded in, so that all that is required is the masking. If not, you will already have marked its position at the bow and stern in order to set the hull up level. The simplest way to mark the line around the hull is to set up a long horizontal straight edge, level with the mark at each end of the hull. They must both extend to at least the full width of the hull and be positioned approximately at right angles to the centreline. Now, as you sight across the two straight edges from a position clear of the hull, so that they are in line with each other, you can get an assistant

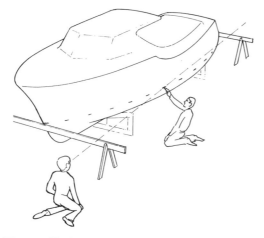

Fig 71 *Marking the waterline. As an alternative to sighting, you can use a cord stretched taut across the boards arranged so that it touches the hull. By changing its position at each end, you will be able to mark progressively around the hull at close intervals.*

to mark the hull with a chinagraph pencil at intervals of about 2ft. You will see clearly, as he puts the pencil to the hull, whether it is high or low, and you can instruct him accordingly.

As he works around, you will have to shift your position to keep his pen point in a sight line with the boards. Using a thin batten, you can join up all the marks with a line, fairing out any odd ones as you go and then apply masking tape above the line. The accuracy can be checked afterwards by sighting across the straight edges at the tape.

If you intend to have a boot-topping above the antifouling, the same technique can be used to obtain the mask line but this should be done before the waterline itself. This will enable you to apply primer to the entire hull below the top edge of the boot-topping. The waterline can then be marked and taped as described.

All fibreglass which has to be painted must first be coated with special self-etching primer. This is a thin, washy solution which provides a key on the otherwise highly polished surface, to enable the paint to adhere. Before application, remove all traces of parting agent and degrease the hull by wiping it over with thinners. After priming, it is wise to apply two coats of *two pot* polyurethane paint before antifouling. This is to give some protection from developing a condition called osmosis, which shows itself as a series of blisters and cracks due to water penetration of the gel-coat. The surface of the polyurethane should be lightly abraded in preparation for over painting with antifouling.

The choice of antifouling depends on local conditions, and how much you are prepared to pay. It is a toxic paint, designed to discharge slowly throughout the season to keep fouling at bay. The price rises in proportion to the strength so find out what type the other owners use in the area. Generally, in colder or more polluted water, fouling of every sort is less vigorous than in warmer or cleaner waters. Also, if you intend to use the boat for racing, the bottom will need cleaning more frequently to ensure maximum speed. The antifouling must therefore be of a type able to withstand scrubbing. On a new boat, two coats will be necessary for the start of the first season, but do not apply the second coat until within a few days of the launching. This is because the effectiveness, particularly of the cheaper paint, diminishes if it is not immersed after a short period.

On deck, the only finish required will generally be gloss varnish. This must be of marine grade. The choice between polyurethane or ordinary varnish is a matter of personal preference but many owners find that overall, the ordinary varnish has better adhesion and the successive coats are less liable to delaminate. Using plain varnish, dilute the first coat with about 10% thinners to achieve good penetration of the timber. Then build the surface up with five or six coats, allowing each one to dry thoroughly and rubbing down lightly with fine sand paper between coats.

Down below, the same varnish and technique can be used but three coats will be sufficient. Many people prefer to use a matt finish, particularly on teak, although these varnishes are not so durable as gloss. To improve the durability and yet achieve a matt finish, it is advisable to use gloss varnish for the first two coats and then coat with matt.

31

Launching

Before you contemplate launching your boat, it is highly desirable to complete all the work down to the last detail. Beware of the temptation to launch in a part-finished state, because it is much more difficult to work with no workshop facilities. Every tool and screw will have to be carried to the boat wherever it is moored and there will probably be no mains electricity available.

Whether your boat is power or sail, you will almost certainly need the engine to take you from the launching site to your mooring, so do not forget to test it well in advance. The initial commissioning of the engine will be described in the manufacturer's handbook. This will include details of the lubricating oils for the sump and gearbox, greasing, fuel priming for diesels, and so on. Fill the fuel tank to see that there are no leaks, and make sure that the exhaust pipe skin valve is open. Engage the gear and crank the engine by hand to check that everything is free. Disconnect the water cooling pipe from the hull inlet valve and place the end in a bucket of water. Disengage the gear, open the throttle and you are ready to start.

Start the engine, and as soon as it is running, cut the speed to a little more than idling. High revs and heavy load must be avoided for the first one hundred hours or so. When it is running smoothly, make sure that the water circulation pump is working by checking the outflow and then see that there is nobody near the propeller and try both forward and reverse gears. Do not leave the shaft running, because the outboard bearing is designed for water lubrication and will be damaged if run dry for more than a few moments.

When you decide to launch, the transport arrangements from your garden to the launching site will generally be a reversal of the original procedure, but you have several other things to organise as well. Where are you going to launch? What time is high water on that day? Will the boat be lifted off the transporter by crane and be put straight into the water, or will it have to be put on to a cradle or slipway first? These are just a few of the things which you need to sort out well in advance to make sure there are no major problems on the day. You will have a great deal to do, so it is generally best to limit the number of people around to just a couple of reliable friends to help. Remember to put sufficient mooring warps, fenders, anchor and chain aboard in good time.

When your boat approaches the water, your handiwork is about to be tested in every way. As soon as she is afloat, go on board with tools and jointing compound so that you can quickly inspect all the valves, pipe work, stern gland etc, to see if there are any leaks and if so, deal with them. Turn all the valves on and check all the equipment. You must ensure that there are no serious leaks while the crane or slipway is still available.

If you have a sailing boat, you will need tools suitable for dealing with the attachment of the lower ends of the rigging. You will of course, have already 'dressed' the mast with all the standing rigging, halliards and spreaders ready to put it up. The main worry at this stage is whether the standing rigging will actually fit when the mast is erected. This seems in practice to be just as uncertain whether you make the rigging yourself or buy a standard professionally-made up set. The problem is far worse if the service of an expensive crane is required to erect the mast.

In order to prepare for these problems, take with you a length of $\frac{1}{4}$in chain, a bundle of $\frac{1}{4}$in galvanised shackles, a hacksaw and a self-grip wrench. These items will enable you to make up the length of any odd wires which may be too short, with either a shackle or two shackles and a length of chain. This arrangement will stay the mast temporarily until you can get aloft to remove the offending wires. Take note of the amount of error and before you remove the wire, attach and set up a halliard to its chainplate as a substitute whilst it is removed for replacement. If there are more than a couple of wires wrong, the mast will have to come down again anyway, but you must ascertain what the error is, in order to get the right lengths next time.

For most owners, the launching is the most traumatic and yet the most joyous part of the whole project. With luck and careful planning it will all run smoothly, bringing your boat to life in her proper environment. She will no doubt give you a great deal of pleasure. In a few years time, as new designs and new ideas emerge, you may again find yourself looking at your tools and contemplating . . . Bon voyage.

32

Tools

Possession of a good range of tools and a decent place to set up a bench are absolute pre-requisites for the task of fitting out a boat. Most people who even contemplate such a job will already be quite skilled with their hands and so, by implication, will probably also have a fair selection of tools. If you do have to buy tools, make sure that they are the best quality that you can afford and then they will not only see the job through but also last a lifetime. It is always false economy to buy cheap tools because they give poor results and have a short life. As a general guide, there will certainly be work for the following tools and possibly a few more.

Mallet	Small, about 1lb
Chisels	$\frac{1}{4}$in, $\frac{3}{8}$in, $\frac{1}{2}$in and $\frac{3}{4}$in widths. Must be good quality with handles suitable for the mallet.
Hammers	$1\frac{1}{2}$lb engineer's ball peine and $1\frac{1}{2}$lb carpenter's claw hammer.
Screwdrivers	$\frac{1}{16}$in (for electrical work), $\frac{1}{8}$in, $\frac{1}{4}$in and $\frac{3}{8}$in
Punch	Small pinpunch (for sinking nail heads)
Planes	2in blade, smoothing (all general work) and a rebate or plough plane if you do not have a circular saw-bench
Drills	$\frac{1}{16}$in to $\frac{1}{2}$in in $\frac{1}{16}$in steps and a rose countersink
Hand drill	General use, also handy for counter-sinking
Saws	Handsaw 8-10 teeth per inch and a tenon saw. A rip saw will also be required if you have no power saw
Square	Carpenter's try-square, about 8in

Rule	Carpenter's four fold 24in
Tape measure	10ft minimum
Carborundum stone	Double graded, coarse/fine for honing all blade tools
Spirit level	2ft long
Plumb bob	Small, but get a proper one, not just a nut on a string.
Spokeshave	Small
Files	10in flat coarse, 8in flat fine, 8in round coarse, 8in half round rasp and 10in flat dreadnought (plastic cutting)
Brace	Carpenter's ratchet type. Can be used for boring holes if no power drill is available, but it will be particularly useful for driving the hundreds of wood and machine screws.
Bits	A few carpenter's bits may well come in useful but if you have an electric drill, use the special, flat power tool bits, say $\frac{3}{8}$in, $\frac{1}{2}$in, $\frac{5}{8}$in, $\frac{3}{4}$in and 1in. They give a good, clean hole and can be easily re-sharpened with a file. Also, a screwdriver bit about $\frac{5}{16}$in, for use in the hand brace will save much effort with screwdrivers.
Pellet cutters	To cut $\frac{3}{8}$in, $\frac{1}{2}$in and possibly $\frac{5}{8}$in diameter for cutting pellets to match the joinery
G-cramps	However many you have, it will not be enough. About four 6in and four 4in will get you by.
Sliding bevel	Not often found in the handyman's toolbox but very useful for transfering angles and bevels from one item to another.
Bench knife	You can buy one with several blades stored in the handle. It will be used mainly for cutting veneers and chopped strand mat. Also purchase one of the special blades for cutting plastic laminate.
Hole saw	You will need to make a variety of different sized holes for the deck and hull fittings. These saws can be purchased either as individual pieces or in a combined set which has interchangeable saws on a common arbor for use in a brace, or preferably an electric drill.
Electric drill	This is the most versatile of all power tools with a wide range of attachments available which convert the drill to tackle other types of machining. Most amateur craftsmen will already possess an electric drill but in order to cope with the heavy torque load imposed when cutting fibreglass, sanding and so on, you will need one of the more powerful ones, or it will not be long before the armature burns out. If you are buying one specially for the job, get one with at least a 400 watt motor and a $\frac{1}{2}$in chuck. It must be double insulated or properly earthed. The simplest and most useful attachment is a sanding disc backing pad. This will be invaluable for general rough sanding and also for use with a tungsten carbide disc for trimming fibreglass. For finishing work, an orbital sanding attachment will give good results, although the plywood faces will not need much attention and the other work is reasonably easy to finish by hand.

A jigsaw attachment will be a reasonable substitute for an independent machine. The main disadvantage is that it needs two hands to control so you have no free hand left to steady the work, as with a separate jigsaw. If you also intend to use your drill to power a circular saw, it will give the best use with a saw bench assembly rather than the hand portable type. In conjunction with this, better work will be produced if you fit a rigid tungsten carbide tipped blade. The capability of the unit will be severely limited by the power of the drill so it will not be very successful in making deep cuts, even in softwood.

Jigsaw This little machine is very useful to the boatbuilder whether amateur or professional. There is a large amount of work cutting out panels and locker doors and also for cutting the window and hatch openings through the fibreglass deck moulding, so again, buy the best you can afford.

You will need a number of blades because they have a short life, particularly when cutting fibreglass. They can be bought in packs with all blades of one type or with a selection of blades. Generally, fibreglass and thicker timber require coarser teeth, but buy a couple of these assorted packs and see how you get on, then you can buy whichever type you require.

Circular saw If you are really taking the job seriously, a circular sawbench capable of cutting 2in deep or more will be in-valuable for all the general sawing, particularly if you are preparing your own timber from larger sizes. It will also produce the timber edging sections very neatly. Best performance and finish will be given if it is fitted with a rigid tungsten carbide tipped blade. This is particularly noticeable in hardwood. The drive motor must be large enough to supply at least $\frac{1}{2}$ HP per inch depth of cut.

Remember, these machines are very dangerous, so use the guards and take no chances.

Engineer's tools You will need a few spanners to suit the nuts under the deck fittings, those involved in the engine installation and the pipework. An engineer's self-grip wrench and possibly also a stilson will be useful. Mechanic's feeler gauges will be necessary to align the engine. $\frac{1}{4}$in, $\frac{5}{16}$in and possibly $\frac{3}{8}$in thread taps and a suitable wrench will be required for the deck fittings.

Index